Emotional First Aid

EMOTIONAL FIRST AID

A Crisis Handbook

Sean Haldane

STATION HILL PRESS

First paperback edition published,1988, by Station Hill Press, Inc., Barrytown, New York 12507. Published by arrangement with Irvington Publishers, Inc. Copyright © 1984

Produced by the Institute for Publishing Arts, Barrytown, New York 12507, a not-for-profit, tax-exempt organization.

Cover designed by Susan Quasha.

Distributed by the Talman Company., Inc., 150 Fifth Avenue, New York, New York 10011.

Library of Congress Cataloging-in-Publication Data

Haldane, Seán.
    Emotional first aid / by Seán Haldane.
      p.   cm.
    Bibliography: p.
    Includes index.
    ISBN 0-88268-071-4 (pbk.)
      1. Emotions. 2. Helping behaviors. 3. Crisis intervention
    (Psychiatry) 4. Reich, Wilhelm, 1897-1957. I. Title.
    BF531.H27 1988
    152.4--dc19

Manufactured in the United States of America.

*For Ghislaine
with love and gratitude*

Contents

1

Emotional First Aid (EFA)

Why emotional first aid?

Emotions are part of the movement of life. It often feels good
to let this movement through. After a good cry or a well-
directed explosion of anger, the whole organism may feel more
alive. But we don't always let these emotions through easily. We
often choke on our tears, or bottle up our anger. Another emotion, fear, stands in the way. We even hold back the most pleasurable emotion—joy.

First aid is temporary relief of distress. Sometimes it is rudi-
mentary medical help before the doctor comes. But quite often
this is enough: a bandaged cut will heal on its own, the massage
of an injured muscle may start a spontaneous cure. Why *emotional* first aid? Because often emotion is experienced with distress. The first aid is not to relieve the emotion, or eliminate it
as if it were a pain. It is to relieve the distress of the emotion
pushing against a block: to let the emotion through. It is not
therapy—or at least no more than the bandaging of a shallow
wound is the practice of medicine. But just as traditional first
aid uses simple medical techniques, emotional first aid uses
simple techniques from therapy. Where emotional distress is
extreme or long lasting, professional help may be necessary. But
often emotional first aid (EFA) is all that is required.

The techniques of EFA are not widely known, and are almost
never consciously applied. They are often applied intuitively,

however, as when a mother comforts her child, or when we let a friend cry on our shoulder. The idea of consciously applied emotional first aid may even be obnoxious to many people: why use a cold, calculated technique instead of warm support? But the technique need not be cold. And there is a real problem: how often do we respond fully to our friends' emotions, how often do we feel our support is adequate?

We often face the emotions of others with an increasing sense of paralysis and distress in ourselves. We tend to take steps to help the other person's unhappiness go away. We tell the person to cheer up, we offer them something to eat, or make casual something that is, after all, being seriously felt. We often have problems with our own emotions. So we tend to consider emotions themselves a problem. Even healthy activities such as jogging or dancing are often used to channel energy away from emotional expression into another kind of more controlled discharge. Or the beginning sensations of rage, fear, or grief are often kept dull by the use of tranquilizers. At worst, emotions may be held in so firmly that the result is physical damage—ranging from a tension headache to chronic psychosomatic disease. In the final analysis, many surgical operations cut out the physical results or the pain of repressed emotions.

Emotions are apparently still not officially respectable in the health sciences. For example, a 2,500 page *Comprehensive Textbook of Psychiatry* contains no systematic study of emotions and, in an index of some 20,000 entries, contains less than thirty entries under 'emotional' or 'emotions.' But many psychotherapists (psychiatrists, psychologists, counsellors) use techniques to relieve emotional distress. They may also try to induce emotions and intensify them. This is often manipulative, or even dangerous, since emotions can be 'dynamite.' Many psychotherapists, since unfortunately their training does not usually include work on their own emotional blocks, fumble just as much in the face of a patient's emotions as the man in the street would. Standard medical and psychological data come from a mechanistic analysis of human or animal behavior. 'Avoidance' or 'aggression' are discussed, rather than fear and anger, since much of the usual data originates in experiments with laboratory rats which must feel emotion but do not show it in ways we recognize as expressive.

Manipulation of the emotions also frequently occurs in the setting of therapy groups or training groups, where in many cases the original honesty of the encounter group concept has been lost. Experienced leaders can take advantage of people's lack of emotional experience by causing dramatic break-throughs which are in effect a breaking down of the person. The leader can then benefit from a surge of love and gratitude in putting the pieces together again. Since the knowledge of EFA is a knowledge of emotional functioning, it may, apart from its immediate value in relieving distress, also provide an inoculation against becoming the easy victim of emotional manipulation.

Most of the techniques used by those psychotherapists who are prepared to work seriously with the emotions derive ulti-mately from the work of Wilhelm Reich. Reich pioneered in leading psychotherapy away from mere listening and talking toward a more intensive contact with the emotional blocks ex-pressed in various body attitudes—for example, a tight jaw that held back crying, or a puffed-up chest that held back rage. It was Reich who first used the phrase 'emotional first aid' to describe help he had given to his own young son who had been bottling up rage after being ill-treated by some other children. Reich remarked that 'teachers and parents should learn to do the same thing,' and 'One must also have a good relationship with one's child. One must have confidence and proper knowl-edge.'

The first aim of this book is to communcate basic knowledge of ways to relieve emotional distress. But this knowledge must be based on the understanding of how emotions function. The pioneer in this field was Charles Darwin. His book, *The Expression of the Emotions in Man and Animals,* published in 1872, is still the most complete available description of the details of emotional expression. He is best known for having broken the taboo against linking human and animal functioning in his theory of the evolution of man from ape-like ancestors. His later study broke another taboo, especially strong in nineteenth-century England, against discussion of the emotions. Darwin described some of his own emotions and some of his psycho-somatic problems, used many photographs (in the first days of the camera) of his children in various emotional states, and gathered data through a questionnaire from all over the world. Essentially, he saw emotional expression as the channeling of energy, which he called 'nerve force.' Reich's emphasis, sixty years later, was even more on the actual movement of a biological 'life energy' in the body. Darwin's observations of detail in expression, and Reich's analysis of how emotions may flow or become blocked, are the reference points in this book's preliminary discussion (Chapter 2) of the dynamics of the emotions, what happens when a person is 'moved.'

Some simple methods taken from Reichian therapy will also be explained. These are not some kind of trade secret, since every patient who has been through therapy will know them. To take a proprietary attitude to such methods would be analogous to the medical profession trying to monopolize the use of bandages or preventing people from touching each other. The only methods from therapy that could be dangerous in themselves (any method can be misused) are those that deliberately intensify an emotional situation. In terms of energy, therapy will often attempt to *charge* a person, to increase tension and excitation. Emotional first aid works mainly in the direction of *discharge,* of release of tension that has already built up.

Having a good relationship with another person cannot be taught. But in the context of EFA, certain guidelines can govern the support to be offered, so that it does not become an invasion of the other person. Support without intrusion (see Chapter 3) can be achieved if intervention is limited by certain basic rules.

Confidence in the face of emotional distress also cannot be taught. But it depends on how much the helper accepts his or her own emotions. When someone else is moved, we are also moved. To give emotional first aid, the helper has to be able to manage his or her own emotions, to accept them, even to share them, while not intruding with them. This book, throughout, offers guidelines for emotional self help.

There may be some objections to this attempt to make emotional expression a more conscious process. It may seem as if this book prescribes behavior: the right way to cry, the right way to get angry. This would be as absurd as defining the right way to make love. But it is possible to discuss the basic process of emotional discharge and, by understanding it, to become more capable of surrender to it, just as it is possible for lovers to become closer to each other through an open discussion of their sex life. Of course, the content and rhythm of each person's experience is unique, but the basic emotions are still universal—if they are allowed to come through.

2

Emotion and Blocks

This chapter explains some general principles of emotional expression and its blocking.

Vertical flow

The head end of any organism is the leading end in movement forward. This is not so obvious in adult humans who spend most of the day standing or sitting up. But we still tend to make contact with the world head first, through the main sensory organs—eyes, nose, ears, mouth. Feelings in response to our perceptions 'register' further down, mainly in the chest or abdomen. Our digestive system also takes in at the head end and eliminates at the tail end. 'Charging' of the body, excited breathing, begins at the head: the mouth opens wide in excitement.

Emotional discharge has either an upward or a downward direction in the body. For example, joy comes flooding up from the heart or abdomen and produces tears in the eyes. The upward rush may be so strong in a child that it will apparently defy gravity and the child will 'jump for joy.' Conversely, a depressed person feels 'down.' Rage also rushes up to the head: a person will 'get his back up.' Fear prostrates the organism: the person tends to collapse downward, to seek the ground. Grief also seeks the ground: a person lies down to cry, but the sobbing comes from chest and abdomen and out the face and eyes.

As a general rule, therefore, emotion can be said to flow up and down in the body.

Horizontal blocking

The vertical flow of an emotion upward or downward can be blocked by muscular holding which forms a horizontal block. If you want to hold back tears, to 'put a brave face' on a situation in spite of the despair pressing upward in your chest for release, you can first try to check the flow by swallowing down the tears, but you will then tend to prevent your tears by tightening your jaw. Since the muscles in the jaw are connected to those of the base of the skull at the back of the neck, a ring of muscle tension is produced which is horizontal to the flow of grief upward.

Similarly, if an emotional impulse in the arms is blocked, to reach outward in longing or to hit out in rage, these movements on the vertical axis can be held by tightening the upper chest and shoulders. This forms a horizontal bar of rigid muscle across the body.

This dynamic was compared by Reich to the functioning of a worm: if one of the horizontal rings or segments of the worm's body were somehow rigid, the flow forward of the worm's movement would be blocked. Reich proposed that in a human, when the vertical flow of emotion was habitually blocked, the result was a chronic 'muscle armor' of horizontal spasms. For example, a child who suppresses crying for many years will develop a rigid, 'grim' jaw, involving spasm of the muscles of the jaw and the back of the neck—in effect a ring of tension. A child taught to suppress pleasure will develop a hard, rigid abdomen, and by extension muscular spasms in the lower back— another ring. Such blocks are often part of a person's 'character structure,' and where they are severe it takes sustained therapy to relieve them. But where they are light, or temporary, or just beginning in a child, emotional first aid may help them let go.

"Yes" and "No" in the body

The equivalent of horizontal blocking in terms of movement is the side-to-side movement that expresses a 'No' in the body, for example the shaking of the head or the waggling of the finger from side to side when saying no, and the predominately side to side movements in wriggling out of the way of a threat. This is the opposite of 'Yes' with the body, which consists of movements *forward:* reaching with mouth or arms, or sighing in acceptance of a soft emotion such as joy or grief, the body folding forward with the outbreath.

In infants, as Darwin noted, the first side-to-side 'No' is observable in the sharp movements of the head when rejecting the mother's breast if it is forced upon an infant who is already satisfied. Modern observers have also noted a very early reaction of avoidance in infants: a rearing back from something unpleasant, with the back becoming locked in an arched position. This may still be seen in some adults who panic under emotion. Arching backward, like side-to-side movments, prevents the folding forward of the body that occurs in any deep surrender or release of pleasurable emotion.

Expansion and contraction

In another comparison of human functioning with that of more primitive organisms, Reich pointed out that an ameba (a microscopic single-celled organism rather like a transparent crawling sponge) will expand in area as it moves out in exploration of its environment, but contract when it meets an obstacle. It protrudes part of its body as a feeler, then retracts it sharply if it meets a hard object. Similarly, the human organism 'expands' in pleasure (we reach out to the world) and 'contracts' in anxiety (we retreat into ourselves).

If pleasure is a soft expansion, anger seems to be a hard expansion. Along the same lines of observation, Darwin pointed out that animals expand in rage: their hair or feathers bristle or puff up, and if possible they adopt a towering posture. In fear, they contract: hair or feathers are flattened, and they cringe near the ground.

Other observers have pointed out that when a baby cries its whole body seems to shrink; when it is angry it becomes puffed up and hard; and when it is experiencing pleasure it expands softly.

Generally speaking, the body shows a soft expansion in joy and a hard expansion in anger, a soft contraction in grief and a hard contraction in fear.

Breathing

Breathing is a pulsation in which expansion and contraction of the body alternate. The simplest way to block the expansive or contractive movement of the body in emotional expression is to suspend the main pulsation in the organism: to hold the breath. Not that this is a conscious process. The jaw clamps shut, or the muscles of chest and abdomen spontaneously tighten as anxiety is felt.

The word *anxiety,* from the Latin word for 'narrow,' expresses this experience of tightness of the muscles of jaw, throat, chest, and abdomen. The channel of breathing is narrowed. Anxiety in its most intense form is fear—a total contraction of the organism. But normally anxiety is a partial contraction against an impending movement of emotion.

When the expansive emotions of joy or rage are blocked, either chronically or in a temporary emergency, the breathing tends to block in a deflated position, with the body area contracted. A depressed person, whose organism resists either joy or rage, tends to be stuck in an attitude of deflation. The body is slumped, hunched, folded forward. The attitude seems to say 'I've given up.'

When the contractive emotions of grief or fear are blocked, the breathing tends to be held in an inflated position, the chest puffed out. The attitude may seem defiant: 'I won't give in.'

Contact

Another way to sever emotion is to sever contact. This occurs mainly through the eyes which can switch off the input from any situation that threatens to charge and excite the person. The most obvious way of doing this is to close the eyes, to deny the experience. But sometimes the denial seems to be at the level of the brain: the eyes do not close but they glaze over and the person 'goes away.' A panicky flickering from side to side or rolling of the eyes also shuts off sustained contact.

Cutting contact does not always work. The brain may produce its own inner phantoms. Nothing is more dangerous, for example, than blind rage.

Emergency reactions

The ways in which a person mainly blocks emotion depend on his or her character structure, which in turn seems to depend on the kinds of emergencies that have been experienced during childhood. The repeated experience of emergency, with its forcible action on the autonomic (involuntary) nervous system, can affect the child's whole body structure. An emergency, for a child, is any threat to its life. Since children are more "alive" than they usually become as adults, any kind of harsh treatment, even if it does not lead to physical death, may have traumatic effects. This life in a child may become stilled in certain areas of functioning, overstimulated and erratic in others. Some common emergency conditions for children are parental coldness, erratic handling, brutal attack, and smothering domination. Depending on when in the child's life such events occur, a basic emergency reaction tends to become established. This is visible in many adults as the immediate, fixed response to *any* emotion-charged situation. For example, grief may seem like an appropriate response to irreversible loss, but in some people the first response is rage, and in others it is panic. Investigation usually reveals that the person would have the same first response to another situation, such as verbal attack. Under attack, the person whose reaction to loss is grief may also react with grief, instead of fighting back. It is not that a given response is necessarily wrong. But the reactions of some people are dominated by only one response.

The number of basic emergency reactions is apparently limited by human biology. There are only a few options:

1. Freezing   (Fright rigidity)
2. Collapse   (Fright paralysis)
3. Clinging   (Flight toward protection)
4. Panic   (Flight away from danger)
5. Attack   (Fight)

Fright rigidity and paralysis are distinguished here for the sake of accuracy: the first implies rigidity of the musculature (hypertonus), the second flaccidity (hypotonus). But for practical purposes, in EFA, both can be considered under the general heading of 'freezing.'

There are also two ambivalent reactions whose origin seems to be in inconsistent experience with parents who one moment give pleasure, the next pain, or even worse, both at once. An example is the double-message situation where a parent clearly feels a sensual contact with the child as pleasurable but at the same time harshly forbids it. The first ambivalent reaction can be called *captive ambivalence:* the person is caught in a struggle between clinging and attack, not sure whether the situation is going to be threatening or pleasurable. The second is *mobile ambivalence,* where there is alternate flight toward and flight away from the situation.

EFA should not attempt to change these basic reactions if they seem excessive. This is a job for therapy, if the person decides this is needed. But it helps to be able to identify the reactions. They can be respected as part of the person's basic structure, and there can be some encouragement to let the underlying emotion surface and take a direction that may move the person out of the emergency, at least temporarily.

Specific emotions

Just as the number of human emergency reactions is limited

to certain basic options, the number of basic emotions seems to be limited to four: grief, fear, joy, and anger—or, soft contraction, hard contraction, soft expansion, and hard expansion.

It might be argued that there are more emotions. Darwin, in his study, discussed surprise, contempt, disgust, shame, and guilt. However, in terms of dynamics these appear to be states, that is, relatively static conditions, rather than clear movements of sensation and energy inward or outward. There is a 'half-way' quality to such states as guilt, shame, and contempt. If intensified they lead to movement in the form of one of the four basic emotions. There is no such thing as a pure emotional expression of guilt or contempt: when mobilized they turn inevitably into grief, fear, or anger. A case might be made that disgust, which has a definitely recognizable expression in vomiting, is a specific emotion. But in its pure form, such as vomiting food, it is a physiological reflex, not an emotion. Nor is it necessarily accompanied by an emotion. When disgust is expressed emotionally, it is a forceful rejection of another person or thing, and is part of anger.

It may be useful in psychological studies to define and label many shades of emotion, but for all practical purposes it is enough to analyze the functioning of the four basic emotions. They are clearly recognizable, and specific EFA measures can be suggested for each of them. The various states— guilt, contempt, etc.—will be discussed only incidentally in this book.

Pleasure and pain are not in themselves emotions, nor are they merely states. They have a function of movement. Pleasure is associated with expansion of the organism, pain with contraction. They seem to be even more basic than the emotions: the two sides of the most primitive pulsation of life, observable in even the most primitive organisms as approach and avoidance. It would be convenient to propose that the expansive emotions of anger and joy are pleasurable, and that the contractive emotions of grief and fear are painful. But, in practice, any emotion can contain a mixture of pleasure and pain. It can be pleasurable to explode in anger, to surrender to crying, or even to give way to panic after a long build up of anxiety. And even joy sometimes contains a nostalgic tug of pain. In general, however, the resolution that follows an emotional outburst is pleasurable. Pain is most acute when an emotion is suppressed.

3

Support without Invasion

When and where

Like medical first aid, emotional first aid offers help but not necessarily cure. Nor does it offer advice on further treatment. Since emotional distress is not a sickness, there is no need to assume a person needs further help once the distress has been relieved. The person can make his or her own decisions about the need for some kind of therapy (see Chapter 9).

EFA is most appropriate where there is already a relationship, since it requires contact and caring. In any good personal relationship, of friend with friend, or parent with child, emotional support is already being given. If distress occurs, the support may turn easily toward emotional first aid without any verbal 'contract' being necessary.

A contract can be as simple as an offer to help and its acceptance by word or gesture. Even among friends it may be best to start with such a contract. In a counseling, teaching, or work situation, where the boundaries of involvement may not have been clearly established, such a contract is always necessary before the further involvement that EFA represents.

The person in distress may spontaneously ask for help. Even here it is best not to rush in. The following section lists some of the dangers.

Invasion

Invasion may occur when the helper loses sight of the distressed person's need. The helper presses his or her own need, and the person becomes a victim. It is as if someone cleaning out a shallow wound dug in with a knife. A problem with EFA is that its abuses are not so obvious as in medical first aid. We are not used to really observing emotions, let alone managing them. And when we do, our observation is often blurred by our own emotional blocks. But some common invasions can be identified:

—*unasked for help,* given when there is not already a personal relationship or a contract that would permit any gesture, such as touching or holding, which the EFA requires.

—*programming* the distressed person, manipulating them into what the helper decides is the most acceptable emotion.

—*doing therapy.* This includes taking measures to increase the tension of the situation, deepening the emotion to breaking point, and delving into private details. All this is best left to a therapeutic context that the person has contracted for.

—*faking concern.* Doing EFA with a person whom you dislike is an invasion, an intrusion of falseness into the person's already difficult situation.

—*relentless contact.* There is a natural pulsation in human interaction, between contact and withdrawal. Relentless contact, not letting go for one minute—of eye contact, talking, touching, or whatever the medium of contact is—is ultimately hypnotic and controlling.

—*stickiness, smothering.* A kind of relentless contact where either the helper's own need for contact is taking over, or some of his or her own resentment is being covered up.

'Third-party emotions'

An important limitation to emotional first aid is that it can only be valid for 'third-party emotions.' That is, if *you* have caused the emotion, you cannot help adequately if it causes distress. You cannot remain objective, and your motives will be

suspect. In the cases of grief and fear, if these emotions in someone else result from something you have done or provoked,
your attempts to help may seem sadistic. In the case of rage,
you will simply be joining battle with the person.

This leaves a wide range of situations where your help can be
needed, where emotional distress is clearly related to situations
for which you are not responsible. There is inevitably a middle
area, where the other person is upset by a situation in which
you are partly involved, or in which you share but are less
upset. In such cases, you can only help validly if you are confident of being able to maintain enough emotional distance to
respect the basic guidelines for noninvasion.

The helper's motives

Why are you reading this book?

You might ask yourself this question and try to follow it
through honestly, in particular searching for the *irrational* elements in your interest in EFA. If you analyze these irrational
elements, this will not get rid of them, but they will at least
come out of hiding and you may then become more aware of
the *rational* elements in your interest: no matter how many irrational elements you identify, rational elements will remain. It is
useful to know them also.

By irrational I mean such personal 'trips' as needing to be a
savior, to be kind, to be powerful, to be a calm rescuer—and
especially to be seen doing these things. There is no shame in
this. Many good therapists have begun as 'rescuers' (for example, fulfilling an old need to rescue a martyred mother), just
as many good parents of children have begun their families to
make up for a lack of love in their own childhood. None of us is
completely clear of these kinds of motives. But it helps to
identify them, since they will influence emotional contact. The
danger is that a distressed person becomes, at the emotional
level, someone from your past, so your action becomes inappropriate.

It may help to ask yourself questions about what kind of
emotional support or help you yourself have received in the

past, and what kind you might need now. What kind of 'help' do you most dislike?, and so on. It is useful to discuss these issues with a friend who will give you some perspective on yourself.

The contact cycle

If two people are in contact during a shared task or a conversation, the contact need not lead to a more deep interpersonal involvement since the presence of a third element, the task or discussion, channels the energy outward. In medical first aid, the physical condition of the distressed person becomes such a third element, as does the conflict or emotional expression of a client in therapy. Much therapy follows the rhythm of a contact cycle: *contact, intensification, release, resolution.* For example, a therapist may start by making contact with the client's problem or conflict, then encourage its intensification to the point that forces a release of whatever has been blocking the resolution that is now able to follow. Throughout this cycle, the therapist must be in contact with the client but, at the same time, keep a certain distance so as to retain some objective judgement of what the client is capable of in the particular session. If a therapist becomes emotionally involved with a client, the therapy goes astray because this objective concentration on a third element, the client's conflict or problem, becomes lost. What is necessary, in therapy and in EFA, is emotional response without emotional involvement.

Contact between two people in which there is no concentration of attention on a third element leads automatically to increased excitation. If you try maintaining eye contact with another person, while not staring, allowing yourself to blink normally, and at the same time you do not restrain your breathing, it is probable that an impulse will emerge toward further contact or emotional expression. You may get angry, or want to embrace the person, to cry, to run away, or to begin some kind of joint activity that will draw the increasing energy off into external movement. Or you may feel increasing anxiety and a sense of constriction as your organism rejects the excitement or emotion. Normally, the contact cycle tends to impose itself automatically when there is no third element. For example, in the case of lovers or of parents and their children, the contact between two organisms can intensify into an embrace and a release of emotion or pleasure. Spontaneous intensification of contact to the point of emotional release also occurs among friends or in special situations such as partings and meetings.

It is important to keep a certain distance during EFA. This is not coldness. You can still be caring, communicate tenderness, and remain in touch with your own emotions. But if the helping situation is lost sight of, and you abandon yourself to unrestrained contact with the distressed person, your problems will take as much space as theirs. You may end up crying together, fighting, making love, or clinging to each other. There is nothing wrong with any of these reactions in themselves. But EFA presupposes that one person is in distress and the other is helping, and once a contract has been made, it requires that you maintain some objectivity.

It may be particularly dangerous to apply any intensifying measures to children or adolescents, who are not as well protected by experience as adults are. Invasion risks harmful consequences. This may be true of many adults as well. Never underestimate a person's vulnerability, even if it is covered over by rage or hardness.

Deliberate intensification measures are not recommended in EFA. But a spontaneous process of intensification of either the emotion or the resistance to it is to be expected if you enter into contact with the person. It is not to be feared. In the chapters on basic emotions, ways will be discussed of handling this intensification and channeling it toward release and resolution.

Maintaining contact

Your capacity to stay in contact with the person and the situation depends on your character structure and your habitual response to emergency. Whatever your structure, however, the signs of increasing nervousness or anxiety tend to be: a diminishing capacity for eye contact, tightness of the breathing, and unsteadiness on the feet if you are standing up.

Eyes. If you feel panicky or your eyes are tending to mist over, move your gaze away from the person and back a few times, and make sure you are blinking normally.

Breathing. If you feel constricted in chest or abdomen, you may be holding your breath or breathing more shallowly than usual. Try to allow your breathing to move in your abdomen as a base, then extend it gently up into your chest so that your ribs move with each breath.

Ground. If you feel shaky on your feet, make sure your knees are unlocked, adopt a more 'ape-like' stance in which you can feel a certain springiness in your knees and more contact with the ground.

Then turn your attention back to the other person. This attention, if it is calm and yet not remote, constant and yet not relentless or overwhelming, is in itself a large part of EFA.

Some *don'ts:*

Don't invade

Don't initiate (Help unblock what is happening, don't make something new happen.)

Don't interpret (Leave analysis for later, if at all.)

Don't redirect (Don't decide that a given expression is incorrect and try to replace it by another.)

Don't 'overcharge' (Don't try to raise a level of excitation that is already difficult to handle.)

Don't prohibit (Unless there is physical danger, let the persson's organism find its own way, using EFA to lead the way where necessary.)

Don't condescend (We are all somewhat like children in our emotional expressions. But a superior view of the distressed person as childish is of no value. Remember that you too have many childlike emotions.)

The basic rule

Finally, the basic rule of all EFA must be: *Never try to help a person to express an emotion that you yourself are not able to express.*

4

Grief

Expression

The face of grief was described by Darwin as having two main features: a turning down of the corners of the mouth, and a slanting downward of the eyebrows obliquely while the centre of the forehead is raised. The expression of forehead and mouth match each other in the turning downward at the edges. We all recognize this. The popular phrase 'down in the mouth' describes it. In crying, the active expression of grief, spasmodic sobs shake the chest and shoulders, and the eyes tend to close tightly as tears are shed. The downward slant of the eyebrows and the corners of the mouth becomes more acute.

Darwin also noted that young infants do not sob, with the characteristic breaks in the outbreath, but instead utter a long unbroken wail. Modern psychologists note that this wail is difficult to distinguish from anger. Its emotional content is essentially a demand for the mother. Broken sobbing seems to begin when the infant becomes aware of the experience of loss: the sound breaks with sadness in the knowledge that the wail may not produce a response. Raging demand and despairing loss both occur in the expression of adult grief.

Where the rage content of crying is high, the expression has a hard quality, and the person may instinctively push away any tender approach from a helper. The energy of the crying is directed quite forcefully outward, and contains long wailing sounds between sobs. In despair, the expression is softer. The sobs do come out, but seemingly from a great depth. They are partly locked up in the abdomen, and the person may be doubled over, 'racked by sobbing.' Outward movement consists of reaching out or clinging with the hands.

Crying mixed with rage is discussed in a later section, *Switching*. If a switch to outright anger does occur, this demands measures discussed in Chapter 5, on anger.

Despairing crying, 'pure grief,' involves soft convulsions of the body: the chest lets down in breathing out and jerks in spasms that shake the shoulders, as the head is pulled backward and the pelvis tends to jerk forward. If the person is lying down, a more or less fetal position of being curled up occurs. Eventually the discharge of emotion is complete, although it may rebound again into new periods of sobbing that in turn subside, leaving the person fresh and relieved—what we mean by such phrases as 'there's nothing like a good cry.' A good cry leaves the body warm, face flushed, eyes bright, chest and abdomen soft and mobile.

The social expression of crying is clinging. This is ultimately like the clinging of a baby to its mother. Even if the person is alone, he or she will tend to cling to a handkerchief or pillow.

Experiencing

You can test some of the measures that will be discussed in this chapter by applying them to yourself. It is also useful to gain some sense of how the encouragement of the movements that occur in an expression may intensify the feeling that is building up. You can, in fact, artificially induce some of the feelings of grief by imitating it. You might try the following exercises a few times. As you become used to them, the feeling may emerge. They can also be used as self-help measures, if you feel a knot of sadness inside that you want to relieve.

1) If you are sitting down, take your face in your hands, palms against your cheeks and fingers over the eyes, and begin to rock back and forth from the waist, at the same time letting out an 'Ooooooh' sound that continues to the end of each out-

breath. Make the outbreath as long as you can, letting your chest collapse inward. You may feel some of the sensations of sorrow, and your chest may begin to make sobbing motions during the outbreath. (If this procedure makes you anxious, take away your hands and look around.)

2) Try to simulate sobbing in whatever way seems suitable to you. In particular, you might lie down on your side in a slightly curled position, imitate the face of grief, and as you breathe out deliberately make your chest jerk by uttering the sound of 'Ah-ha, a-ha, a-ha.' Always breathe out all the way. Act it out, let it be dramatic.

3) Try lying on your back with your knees up and feet flat (a position that frees the abdomen) and looking around the walls of the room for a few minutes, in a lonely, searching way, while letting out deep sighs.

4) In the same position, clutch a cushion tightly against your chest, and sigh out deeply making an 'Oooooh' sound, squeezing your eyelids tight with the outbreath, relaxing them but not opening them on the inbreath.

If you find yourself crying, give in to the feelings, and don't be ashamed. We all have something to cry about.

Distress

What happens physically in the full expression of an emotion contains the clues about how the expression may be blocked, whether by a temporary resistance to it or by a longstanding trait of character structure. Since in crying the head moves back in an attitude of surrender, and the chest lets down convulsively, resistance to crying implies a stiffening of the back of the neck and a hardening of the chest in an inflated position. Similarly, the throat may tighten against letting out a sigh (the person may choke back the tears) and the shoulders may be held high and rigid, which prevents any shaking. In many people who have been left to 'cry it out' as infants, or who have hardened themselves against seeming too soft, the abdomen has become hard and tight—a common block against deep feelings that have become too painful or shameful to endure. EFA can help dissolve these resistances and muscular tensions if they are not too deeply ingrained.

Some outward signs of distress that accompany the grief expression when a person is feeling the need to cry but suppressing it are:

—The eyes stare, without making contact, in an expression of despair. (If you know the person well enough to be sure that the pupils are normally mobile, a fixed dilation of the pupils is a sign of anxiety or of impending crying; after crying the pupils regain their mobility.)

—The mouth is clamped shut in an expression of misery, sometimes so forcefully that the lips may pucker or whiten.

—'Freezing.' The body is held stiffly, the chest immobile and inflated. Often some tears in the eyes are the only indication of emotion.

—There is agitation or panic while the grief expression is visible on the face. Sometimes the person will look 'about to burst'—chest inflated, hands tense, shoulders high.

—Rocking the body back and forth over a narrow range may be visible, while the body itself is held immobile and tight.

—The voice becomes low and monotonous, with apparent difficulty in speaking.

As a person begins to cry, signs of blocking are:

—choking sounds, sometimes severe enough to become retching and spluttering.

—hardening and stiffening of chest and neck.

—attempts to hold the breath: the mouth clamped shut, with convulsive swallowing 'bottled in.'

—Dry sobbing. The eyes do not participate. Instead they stare, or if shut, there are no tears.

Provocation

It is unnecessary to explore (as will be the case with anger and fear) ways to provoke the emotion of grief, since these are obvious—cruelty, withdrawal of support, and so on. But it may be worth noting that efforts to impose an ethic of 'don't cry,' 'be brave,' or 'let's put a brave face on it,' may, paradoxically, provoke an explosion of grief. If you want to test this, you might try sticking your jaw forward defiantly and saying out loud: 'I *won't* cry, I *won't* cry.' Chances are you will begin to feel very sad.

Contact (1): Words

The first stage of contact must be through words, but it is advisable to keep them brief. The content will not likely be heard anyway if the person is deeply distressed. The timing of when to speak and make a tentative contract for help is up to you—it depends on how well you know the person, or what the needs of the situation are. If you don't run from the pain of your own concern, and you stay serious, you will find the right thing to say. Simple comments like 'it must really hurt,' or 'you must feel very bad about it,' provided they are not made in a condescending way, may help the emotion spill over. They legit-imize and confirm the person's feeling and give a permission, which may be needed, to express it. And there are simple ques-tions or suggestions such as 'Can I help you?', 'Will you let me hold you?' or 'It's O.K. to let it out.'

It is best to restrict your words to simple descriptions of what you see or feel. Forget, for a while, discussion of the con-tent of the person's problem. Even once the person has agreed to let you help, stick to descriptions, even of resistances. 'You're holding yourself so tight; let yourself breathe.'

The person should also be encouraged to express his or her feelings nonverbally. Don't prohibit talk, but suggest alterna-tives: 'Why not just lie down over here and let go.' Encourage the person to sigh, to make sounds rather than form words.

Finally, if the person refuses your help, take no for an an-swer. If you are concerned, of course stay around in case you can give physical support such as helping the person into an-other room, or finding something to drink or a blanket—what-ever is necessary. But don't push emotional contact, once it has been refused, unless the person changes his or her mind and asks for it.

Contact (2): Touch, Movement

Whether you touch the person must, again, depend on the relationship you already have. But if the person has accepted your offer of help, gentle touch will probably also be acceptable. Again, take no for an answer. If the person stiffens or freezes when you touch, it is best to stop.

There are obvious gestures of support: letting tenderness show in your eyes, taking a person's hand, putting your arm around the person's shoulders, giving a comforting squeeze, holding the person, even rocking them gently. Some gestures may be more specifically directed to areas of muscular holding. Even laying the hand gently on such an area may lead to some letting go:

—If the person is lying down and crying, it helps to lay your hand gently on the back of the neck and keep it there for a while. This encourages surrender of the muscles that may hold the head stiffly.

—If the person seems embarrassed to cry in front of you, it helps to take their hands gently and place them so that they cover the face and eyes.

—Laying your hand on the person's head is often helpful.

Here are some more active measures:

—Massage with your fingertips the scalp, the temples, and the face, pulling the skin in a downward direction. (You have to have a fairly intimate relationship with a person before being able to touch them on the face.)

—Encourage the person to lie on the side in a fetal position holding a cushion or their knees, and massage the back of the neck, exerting a little extra pressure each time he or she breathes out, so as to help the head fall back slightly.

—If the person seems embarrassed or very stiff, ask them to lie on their front, then press firmly down on the muscles of the upper back beside the spine each time they breathe out. Don't apply pressure on the spine itself, nor as far down as the kidneys (the area of the waist). And don't push against any really stiff resistance. This is like artificial respiration: you push down to help the person expel air and sigh out fully. Try and find the breathing rhythm and push to accentuate it, firmly but not harshly. Encourage the person to sigh loudly. The sound 'Oooh' tends to open the throat. But the danger of this active helping of breathing is that the impulse to cry will become more severely caught in the throat, and a dry choking sound may emerge. *Never push against this block,* i.e. do not try to force deflation of the person's chest. (See the section on *Problems* for a discussion of what to do if the person has a tendency to choke on the rising emotion.)

—It may help to urge the person to pause for a few seconds at the end of the outbreath. Press gently on the lower ribs and say something like: 'Don't breathe in too quick. Let yourself feel it.'

—You may notice a grimace or smile on the person's face, holding back the crying tightly. This is not something to work on forcefully, but if you have your hand on the back of the person's neck, reach around the jaw with your thumb or fingers and press gently into the person's cheek. This may dissolve the grimace and let the sobs through. You can maintain this position of your hand to prevent the grimace from coming back: the aim is to encourage the mouth to be open with the lips forward.

—If the person is sobbing but there are no tears, ask them to close their eyes and squeeze the lids tightly shut each time they breathe out.

—It may help to massage the muscles between the neck and the point of the shoulders. But remember, these muscles can be painfully sensitive. You can also take the shoulders in your hands and shake them softly for a moment to help to induce the shaking movement that comes with crying.

—If you already have an intimate relationship with the person, you can massage the area above the navel, just below the ribs. Again, this can be a tender or painful area.

Finally, if the person is a lover or close friend or relative with whom there is no danger of close contact being an invasion or a seduction, hold them as closely to your own body as you can. Grief needs to cling. You can embrace the person quite tightly and pull their chest against your chest as you breathe out. Let your own feelings mingle with theirs, which is natural in this kind of holding. Hold their head against your shoulder with one hand on the back of their neck.

But be careful not to force this on the person. If you feel resistance, withdraw. There may be anger beneath the crying, or a simple need to be alone.

Switching

The main switch of emotions while crying is from grief to anger. Signs that this is happening are: clenching of the fists, tearing at clothes or other available material, or a physical lashing out. The sound may become harsh and bitter, through clenched teeth. (Some societies encourage traditional rites of mourning in which rage at a person's departure into death is apparent in gestures such as the mourners tearing at their own hair and clothes—a process of 'retroflection,' turning back anger onto the self.)

This anger may evoke less tender feelings in you than soft crying, but it is best to encourage it, though without pushing it too far. The best encouragement is acceptance, which you can express verbally. If the person is lying down and you are already applying some pressure to the back or shoulders, you can increase the pressure firmly.

If full scale rage develops, again don't push it, but accept it, taking measures to direct it safely, as outlined in Chapter 5, on Anger. If the person is lying down, don't encourage them to stand up. They (and you) are safer where they are.

A switch from grief to fear is common if a person is crying because of loss. In particular, a person who has been left by a lover, or whose lover has died, may fluctuate between feelings of grief and panic. Proceed as outlined in Chapter 6, on Fear. Since crying is already under way, encourage return to the grief, at least until some of the energy is discharged and there is space to talk rationally about the fears.

Resolution

Many people after crying 'come back' too quickly, overtaken

by a sudden sense of shame, of having made a fool of themselves. They wipe their eyes, sit up briskly, attempt to push the
sorrow aside, then almost inevitably collapse into new sobs a
few minutes later. If this happens, don't attempt to stop it. But
you can take some measures to help the person come back more
slowly, once you see crying beginning to subside:
 —It helps to cover the person with a blanket or coat, then sit
nearby or hold their hand.
 —The person may be pampered for a while. He or she is probably feeling like a fragile child, and may be treated like one.
 —Don't talk about the content of the person's experience for
a while. Restrict your comments to remarks that soothe and
comfort.
 —Reassure the person verbally if they are made anxious by
any involuntary movements and seem to be trying to stiffen
against them; it is natural after any deep discharge of emotion
to tremble and twitch spasmodically.
 Only when the person is calm again is it wise to try to cheer
them up. Test their readiness for this by smiling. If your smile is
returned, the person is probably feeling quite good. In fact,
after the discharge of crying, warm and positive feelings, even
joy, may be experienced. These may cause guilt, since they do
not fit the normally expected program. Actually, there is ambivalence in most feelings. An example of this is grief at losing a
lover, but at the same time a more or less hidden sense of excitement at having new freedom to look for another partner.
Without pushing to turn a feeling around and expose its 'flip
side,' it is important to accept warmly whatever new emotion
emerges during resolution, no matter how surprising it may be
at first. It is often in this transition from one emotion to a new
one, which is in fact emerging from where it has been hidden,
that the person's organism can adapt spontaneously to new circumstances.
 Reich is said to have remarked to a patient who was crying in
a therapy session: 'These are your best moments.' It is true that
deep, soft sobbing, with its surrender to feelings of tenderness
and despair that have often lain buried since childhood, returns
the organism for a while to something like the fresh and vital
state it may have enjoyed before various social pressures and

cruelties forced it to develop an 'armor.' If the person does not sweep the episode of grief under the rug and dismiss it as babyish (the way most of us have been conditioned to do), he or she may retain some of this new found softness, which will make any new experience potentially more vibrant.

Problems

There are several problem situations with the expression of grief that may cause the helper anxiety, but are not dangerous.

Acting out. This is difficult to distinguish. But some people do enjoy being carried away by an enthusiastic expression of grief, to the point where it is being used as a safety valve that prevents the tension building up for the expression of a less socially acceptable emotion—usually anger, but sometimes joy (a hidden pleasure that the mourned person is out of the way). Unless you are a counsellor or therapist, it is not up to you to decide whether the emotional expression you are witnessing is this kind of acting out. But, of course, you have a right to evaluate your own involvement in the situation. If you sense something phony or unreal in the person's grief, you may not feel like helping. On the other hand, the acting out may turn into a more genuine expression. A long period of wailing may not get anywhere, but if it turns to sobbing, the feeling is real. A rule of thumb is to follow the basic principle of taking the person seriously. Follow the progression of the emotion, at least for a while.

Self pity. Like acting out, this may try your patience. Since self pity is a normal part of grief, it can be encouraged at first, but if it continues for a long time and you feel yourself getting angry, it may be worth at least getting some of your anger out briefly. This may bring out any underlying anger in the person as well. Don't use your own anger manipulatively. Be yourself, and be guided by your own feelings. But remember that if you are in an EFA situation, you owe it to the other person to restrain your own feelings if they threaten to take up more space than the other person's.

Freezing. See the earlier section on distress. This may be a serious condition. If several attempts at contact with a person who is seriously frozen do not work, leave the person alone. Don't become angry—the freezing is often covering grief so acute and deep that the person cannot share it without opening feelings of disintegration or dying. In some cases, a stubborn freezing contains elements of angry provocation—the person is waiting for you to make angry attempts at contact so that self-pitying crying or anger can be justified by *your* actions. If you sense this, don't take the bait. But again, if you do not know the person well, it is best to play safe by taking them seriously.

Where you feel the freezing covers a serious grief or pain, you can give passive support by remaining near the person and being available for whatever they may need. If you occupy yourself quietly with your own business, rather than attack the person with incessant smothering attention, he or she may thaw out and ask for something.

Endless hysterical sobbing. Where sobbing involves convulsive movements of the chest, a full discharge of the emotion will eventually occur. In cases of severe loss and mourning, the sobbing will only stop when the person is exhausted. Cover the person with a blanket, or put them to bed. Infinite patience is needed.

Choking. If the person's throat becomes seriously constricted, accompanied by choking sounds, encourage them to turn the choking *outward;* they can take a towel, or your arm, in their hands and 'choke' it by twisting their hands hard and maintaining the pressure while breathing in and out. This action tends to release the constriction in chest and throat.

Emergency. See the section on panic in Chapter 5, *Fear,* for any situation where the person is agitated and mobile while being self-destructive—for example, running around the room and crashing into objects. Self-destruction in grief is usually aimed at either the head or the chest area, where the pressure of emotion bursting toward discharge is too great. The person may, even while lying down, attempt to bang their head against a wall, as if breaking the head open will relieve the pressure. Or they may tear at their clothes or skin in the region of the heart where they feel bursting sensations, as if they could tear open a way for the pain to come out. If there is no medical help immediately available and the person is beginning to do themselves physical damage, you are justified in taking serious measures:

—Restrain the person physically. If it is difficult to hold them still in a protective embrace, try to maneuver them to a bed or the ground and hold them lying down on their front. Lie over their back with your chest if you can do this without exerting a crushing weight.

—If the person is silent but struggling, try to encourage them to yell; this will provide an exit valve for the energy that they feel as bursting. Pinching the cheeks firmly between the fingers and thumb of one hand may provoke yelling, and does not cause damage.

—If there is a period of calm in which the person is able to accept your instructions, ask them to stick one finger down their throat until they gag. Have them do this several times. They will probably not vomit, but the gagging relieves the anxiety and the bursting feelings.

—Try to channel headbanging toward a soft surface, such as a pillow. This is better than trying to stop it.

—If the person is tearing at his or her clothes, make sure they are loose around the neck.

This is short term emergency. In some cases a long term emergency occurs, especially where mourning after a death or a personal loss continues over several months. The person may become exhausted from days of sobbing, the muscles may ache, and there may be no appetite.

This is a difficult problem. In certain primitive societies, mourning is institutionalized and there is a tradition of support from large numbers of friends or relatives and of help and sharing in discharges of grief. In our technological society, mourning tends to be treated as something which should be eliminated. Tranquilizers are used as a kind of chemical surgery of such 'negative' emotions as anger, fear or grief, although unfortunately cutting these emotions out of the organism cuts out much of the capacity for joy and pleasure as well. Some people go onto tranquilizers after a death or separation or marriage break-up, and never come off them. Others, when they do come off after some months of tranquilizers, seem to be haunted by feelings of emptiness and guilt. Or else they plunge again into the emotional crisis which the tranquilizers leave temporarily suspended. A similar situation occurs for many mothers after childbirth in which extensive anesthesia has been used: the person has existed or survived through an event rather than *lived* through it. Post partum depression (or rage) is routine.

Thus, our society does not provide a good context for long-term emotional support. (Such a context, for example, might be 'half way houses' for people in emotional distress, in which they could share their emotions with other healthy people without being diagnosed as ill.) Unless such support is available, the person may have to seek or be referred to medical help—which means, in effect, chemical help. You may feel guilty about encouraging a person in this direction, but you have to honestly assess your own capacity to help. If continuing emotional support of another person in distress threatens your own emotional health, you should feel free to try to find others to share the task with you. You can either let your own emotions emerge, or you can restrain them. Of course, restraint is often necessary and not harmful (see Chapter 5 on *Anger*). But continuing restraint does not eliminate an emotion. It simply turns it inward. The danger of long-term care for someone else is that you may feel consumed by repressed anger and frustration. No matter how much you love a person, you must be able to take at least some breaks for yourself. If they love you, they will understand this in spite of their own distress.

5

Anger

Expression

The basic expression of rage that Darwin noted in both primates and humans consists of a rush of blood to the face and scalp; a 'contraction and lowering of the brow;' a piercing, focused expression of the eyes including constriction of the pupils; eyes fiery and protruding from their sockets; dilation of the nostrils; and the drawing of the lips away from the teeth to reveal them in a snarl, as the breath is pumped in and out between clenched teeth. Darwin was fascinated by the primitiveness of this expression, although he noted that in humans it was usually only visible in young children and in the inmates of mental institutions, who were incapable of controlling it. In most adults it only survived as a frown, concentration of the eyes, dilation of the nostrils, and a clenching of the jaw. The jaw would also be thrust forward, along with the arms and the whole upper part of the body. As Darwin remarks: 'Few men in a great passion, and telling someone to begone, can resist acting as if they intended to strike or push the man violently away.'

Darwin noted that children, like young apes, 'when in a violent rage roll on the ground on their back or bellies, screaming, kicking, scratching, or biting everything within reach.' In adults 'the desire, indeed, to strike becomes so intolerably strong, that inanimate objects are struck or dashed to the ground.' But he also noted that when the muscles are not moving in an angry action, the whole muscular system will tremble. The eyes, too, instead of being focused beneath an intense frown, may be opened very wide in a stare, and instead of the face being flushed and red from the rush of blood to the head, it may become pale as the blood withdraws from the skin surface. Darwin did write of 'the mingled emotions of rage and terror,' but did not have enough of the physiological knowledge that we now have of the autonomic nervous system to realize that the paleness and contraction of the circulatory system are part of 'emergency' functioning. They suggest fear, not anger. The opening wide of the eyes, along with the raising of the forehead is, as Darwin himself notes, an expression of acute fear.

In energy terms, the two 'hard' emotions of fear and anger can be seen as two phases of an emergency situation, with fear as a 'charge stroke' and anger as a 'discharge stroke.' The expression of fear serves to *take in* the emergency situation, and is strictly speaking not so much an *ex*pression as an *im*pression. The expression of anger is a discharge *outward* of energy in the form of threat or aggressive action to remove the obstacle that the emergency has presented. This may become clear in the following short table:

	FEAR	ANGER
Eyes and forehead	Eyes wide open, pupils dilated, forehead raised; eyes staring, glazed.	Eyes pushing forward, focused, pupils constricted, bright and piercing. Forehead bunched into frown.
Mouth and jaw	Mouth wide open, gaping, jaw dropping back.	Mouth clenched, jaw thrust forward.
Circulation	Paleness; contraction of blood supply to center.	Redness; expansion of blood supply to skin.
Hands and arms	Hands open wide, shoulders back in an attitude of being overwhelmed. (Someone 'coming out with their hands up' adopts a stylized version of this expression.)	Hands clenched, shoulders pushed forward in aggression.

The importance of being able to distinguish these expressions is in the fact that when they are mixed they are a better clue to what the person is really experiencing than anything the person may say. If a person utters furiously angry words while his eyes and mouth are wide open, his forehead raised, and his skin pale, he is at the least more frightened than angry. The eyes play a major role in this: in panic, the eyes widen and stare and apparently take in too much of the emergency situation so that the brain becomes overloaded and, in a sense, the person stops really seeing the situation. By contrast, anger is extremely focused in the eyes: an angry person can usually throw an object exactly where he or she wants it to go, or smash a stick against exactly the aimed-for place.

It is when an element of fear is present that the anger begins to become blind and the person lashes out wildly. Children do this in their tantrums because normally the situation is too overwhelming for them, far out of their control. Similarly, an adult's anger becomes blind when indignation is too overwhelming, the enormity of the situation is out of control, or the person is humiliated, back to the wall, with no way out. *There is nothing more dangerous than blind rage.* EFA must concentrate as a first step in not provoking a person to the point at which rage becomes blind (see section on Provocation), or as a second step, where the rage is already blind, trying to reduce the emergency of the situation to proportions on which one can focus. The first step consists of recognition and prevention, the second of channeling and reduction.

Experiencing

If you can find a place where you can be in private and make noise, you might try to explore the following:

—Stage a temper tantrum. Lie down on a soft surface and kick and pound and yell. Get a feel of how unfocused and diffuse this kind of rage is. Just be like a child.

—Standing up, take a rolled newspaper in one hand and hit a hard object viciously, such as the back of a chair. With each blow, let out a loud sound. Keep your mouth open. Roar, make angry faces. Stick out your jaw. In particular, experiment with your eyes: Open them wide and raise the eyebrows in an expression of fear. Keep hitting. Notice how powerless your blows begin to feel, how you lose focus.

—Frown, bunching up the muscles in the center of your forehead, and narrow your eyes to concentrate in a hard glaring look on the point at which you are aiming. Notice how this tends to bring out a real sense of rage.

—With a friend you trust, set up an angry dialogue. A guideline for safety is to agree to stand always in one spot and *under no circumstances move your feet.* In this way, your partner is sure of being able to keep a safe distance. Facing each other, shove at each other with one hand, pushing the palm against the partner's shoulder and saying something like, "Get out of my way!" Again, experiment with the expression of your eyes, to get a feel for how anger may become mixed with fear and lose its focus. Resist the temptation to smile or laugh. (Many people, even when genuinely angry, smile, which establishes a horizontal block against the surge of anger upwards.)

—Grasp a towel tightly in both hands and rotate your fists in opposite directions in a twisting motion. Push your jaw forward and breathe forcefully. You may notice that the harder you twist, the more easy it is to breathe. Or you may feel your throat begin to tighten and your hands lose their strength. Where the capacity for anger is blocked, it is as if we choke ourselves rather than the towel. Try turning the anger outwards, into your hands.

—Seize a towel between your teeth and bite it angrily, making growling sounds. Explore this primitive, childish side to anger. You may feel quickly nauseated. See if you can overcome this by biting hard, growling, and sticking your jaw forward. Again, blocked anger is often displaced into nausea. (See Switching.)

Although some therapies and encounter groups use these experiencing techniques for emotional release, they are not an end in themselves. I am not suggesting that you do 'anger exercises,' which defuse anger from its real object, provoke it unnecessarily, or become a substitute for real-life situations. Simply, you may try these movements a few times in order to test the expression of anger and get a feel for how different expressions evoke or channel different feelings.

Distress

Violence is not treatable by EFA. There is no pat remedy for stopping it once it occurs, and it would be irresponsible to suggest any. It has to be stopped *before* it occurs if possible. The section on Provocation discusses this.

EFA can deal with distress associated with blocking of acute anger—the rage that rises to the surface and becomes held, or that lashes out indiscriminately instead of being focused. There is another kind of distress associated with chronic anger, where a perpetual state of simmering or smouldering resentment is either held in a chronically muscle-bound rigidity of the whole body, or where it is discharged partially by constant complaining or irritability. EFA with anger can work in the following areas:

—to channel and focus destructive anger where it belongs, helping it to remove the real obstacles to a person's functioning.

—to reveal chronic resentment and identify its cause.

—to break the vicious circle in some relationships of provocation by one partner, rage from the other.

—to reduce the occurrence of anger by allowing it, when it does occur, to be more complete.

—to unblock the fear of other people's anger (even when it is not violent), since this fear is often in the last analysis a fear of one's own possible anger.

It is easy to forget that anger has a biological function, of aggressive attack to remove obstacles. In many societies, people are taught to persuade and negotiate or placate rather than to attack obstacles coming from another person. There is a place for this. But paradoxically, it is most easy to exercise the control of anger that negotiation requires, if we are also at times capable of anger. The psychosomatic costs of repressed anger are high, including not only a build up of a muscle armor to prevent explosions, but according to some specialists, a variety of diseases. Many of us repress anger at work and go home to take it out on our families, as a safety valve. But this is destructive. Part of EFA with anger must be to help a person whom society denies the right to be angry at work, to discharge the anger in a focused way.

Much work with anger aims to focus it, to direct it toward specific obstacles, more in keeping with the original biological functioning. The blind rage of violence contains a large element of fear. It is like an animal lashing out blindly in panic. Frightening or dangerous as the situation may be, the person, like an animal in panic, needs to be reassured, calmed, and focused. The danger is unfortunately increased if measures to calm a person are perceived as an intrusion, or even an attack. EFA may aim at times to calm a person, but can only be effective if the anger is accepted. A focused outburst of rage may have to precede the calm. And it may have to be focused at the helper. An understanding of the function of the eyes in the expression of anger is necessary.

Another paradox is that anger directed toward you is, in a sense, a gift. On a personal note, I remember being moved when a therapist once said to me "Give me your anger," when I had been bursting with resentment. I was moved, but also angry, and I certainly 'gave' it. I hurt the other person with what I said, but respected him for having been able to take it. Of course, it hurts to receive anger. It may provoke grief or anger in you. But ask yourself: would you really prefer to have a person you like in a long-lasting state of repressed resentment, sulkiness, or spite, or would you prefer to live through those few painful minutes of receiving the full force of his or her rage? If anger is not violent or too frequent, it is something to be grateful for. Again, it removes an obstacle to the contact between two people.

Some signs of distress when acute anger is being blocked are:

A: Before the explosion

—Fixed respiratory inflation. This is the look of imminent explosion, when the breathing is held, the shoulders pulled back, the neck stiffened. The person may even physically move back or lean back in the chair if sitting down, in an attitude that is the reverse of any angry lunging forward. All this may be under control, but when combined with some of the following other signs of "clamping down" in the face and hands, or with increasing redness of the face, a spring forward in rage is imminent.

—Clenching of the fists, perhaps alternating with unclenching.

—Increasing clamping of the jaw. 'Working' of the jaw as if chewing.

—Reddening of the face, along with a puffy look.

—A scowl of the forehead that increases and then becomes rigid.

—Increased immobility and tension of the musculature.

B. During the explosion

—Agitation, pacing, wild flashing of the eyes, and wild gestures while talking incessantly. This is an intrusion of 'flight' reactions into the basic anger 'fight' reaction, and if allowed to run its course may at least discharge the accumulated tension. Usually it alternates with wild lashing out, either verbally or physically, which EFA may help focus.

—Intrusion of the 'fright' expression on the face: eyebrows raised and eyes opened wide. This often accompanies attempts to convince or persuade or deny that the person is really upset by the situation. It may be a cover for fear.

—Misplaced violence. Random destruction of objects or striking out at other people. Anger directed at anything that happens to be in the way.

Provocation

Anger may provoke anger, and a heated confrontation between two people may end up clearing away a common obstacle in the form of a misunderstanding or accumulated resentment. But often, within intimate relationships, and occasionally in the work context, one person may consistently provoke another. The provoker very often has a problem with the expression of his or her own anger. Provocation is often masochistic. Reich refuted Freud's original theory of masochism as a desire for pain, by pointing out that no living organism really seeks unpleasure. Rather, the masochist is the prey of an unbearable tension for which he or she is unable to find release except through the action of another person. It is like a balloon about to burst that has to seek to be exploded by a pinprick from an outside source. The unbearable tension of the masochist most often contains rage that is blocked and cannot be released. The masochist whines and complains and provokes a person whose rage is more free flowing until that person can no longer stand the provocation and explodes, releasing the tension that has built up in the masochist. Many battered spouses, in particular, report a sensation of relief after being abused.

Without being fullblown masochists, most of us have experienced the sensation of unbearable tension in circumstances where our rage cannot burst out. Think, for example, of how you would behave after two hours in a line up for a plane departure. Most likely, circumstances would not permit an outburst of rage, but your complaints would be insistent and ultimately infuriating to anyone around you. Any person who has grown up in circumstances of constant humiliation, feeling crushed and impotent as if in a perpetual line up, will tend to develop a character structure in which rage is suppressed and replaced by provocative behavior.

A way of identifying your more subtle provocation of anger in others is to examine carefully the last time someone exploded in anger at you. The first question you might ask yourself is: was I angry *before* he or she showed anger? If you were, but did not show it, what were you in fact showing? Were you making any 'digs,' were you whining, were you pretending not to understand something, were you suffering? Were you 'feeding' the other person's anger with new material, facts, or insights that added fuel to the flames? Were you 'rubbing it in,' emphasizing the other person's humiliation in a case where he or she felt abused by someone else? (A sense of impotence or humiliation is further fuel for anger.) What was the expression on your face?

This is not to say that you must always accept responsibility for another person's anger. But since anger is part of an emotional dialogue, it may help to examine your own role in the dialogue before you become indignant at another person's anger. A final question: do you feel secretly relieved when the other person finally does explode? If so, you are passing to that person the responsibility for releasing *your* tension. Most of us do this at times.

Contact (1): Words

In the case of third-party anger, the most important gift you can offer is acceptance. When the anger is distressing, and the person is sounding off verbally or making restless signs of imminent explosion, an attempt to calm the person and make the anger go away will play into a sense of impotence that may be fueling it. The person may calm down but bottle up resentment, some of which may become displaced against you. Instead, accept. 'Sympathize,' in the sense of 'feeling with' (which is what 'sympathy' originally meant in Greek). Mobilize some of your own anger at the situation he or she is describing, without, of course, letting it take more space. This way you help the person feel that the anger is legitimate—which it is, emotionally, no matter what 'reason' might say. Reason can only have space after the emotions have been allowed some discharge.

Use words sparingly, but use them to help the person *focus* the anger. In words, as in gesture, the tendency is for anxiety to become mixed in and for the anger to take off in the direction of incoherent, generalized rage for which the whole world is held responsible. You can focus with words by referring to detail, or asking specific questions: what *did* the third party say? Did he or she really say *that?* Does this situation really mean *this?* And so on. What is sometimes casually referred to as 'the enormity of the situation' is what pushes a person toward panic and thus blind anger. EFA aims to reduce the situation to manageable, less frightening proportions. Help the person focus on detail, using the data he or she has already provided. It may be one or two specific details in the third party's behavior, a vicious phrase or insulting gesture, that really rankle beneath the anger. But caution: Some final detail now remembered may prove to be 'the last straw' and increase at a quantum rate the enormity of the situation.

It is not provocation to make a deliberate attempt to spark a person's anger if they are stuck in a sulk or a state of morose resentment. Some people, usually when in their childhood the expression of anger has been forbidden and monopolized by parents or other family members, lack permission to let anger out. Instead, they turn the anger inward, let it consume them, and become increasingly depressed. If you live with such a person, the whole atmosphere stagnates with a sense of pressure as the person seems to contract away from contact with the world under the burden of unexpressed anger. It is tempting to react to this with your own anger, which may prove to be the needed spark of permission, but may on the other hand add to the person's burdened feeling that the world is against him or her. It is best to confront the person before your own anger builds, and encourage him or her verbally to get angry. 'Doesn't the situation make you feel mad inside?', and so on. But don't nag them with this.

Finally, words are the only way to make a contract for safety if a person's anger is turned toward you, as may happen if you are intimate with the person even when the anger has been triggered by a third party or outside event. The moment this happens, if you wish this to remain an EFA situation instead of becoming an all out battle in which you become equally involved (nothing wrong with this in itself), you can try to set guidelines for the discharge of the person's anger that keep it from getting out of control. The kind of attitude you might express is: 'Look, I know you're getting angry at me, but I just don't want to get hurt. Let's set some rules.'

The best rules limit physical contact: 'You stand there and I'll stand here, then let's say what we want.' Anger expressed just out of arms' reach may be intensified by frustration, but it can work itself through, since gestures of shaking fists or growling or shouting can be made more safely. If your head is cooler than the other person's, you can set the scene. A good rule if you are frightened of the other person's anger, and they too have a frightened look, is for you not to remain standing up, but to sit down. This may seem like a frightening idea, since the person may tower over you and threaten you. You are certainly abandoning some ground in doing this, and it is a gesture of appeasement. But it makes sure that you are not felt to be threatening. If both of you are already sitting down, sit a bit lower in your chair, give the person a bit of height over you. The essence of rage reduction is fear reduction.

Contact (2): Touch, action

EFA in anger has the double function of preventing it from getting out of hand and becoming violent, and at the same time of helping it, as in any emotional discharge, express itself fully. The first part of this function, if it is to succeed, must largely do so through the kind of containment measures mentioned already—avoiding provocation, focusing attention in detail so as to reduce its range, and trying to set up a physical situation in which you are not threatening to the person and you are out of physical reach while remaining within emotional reach.

The second phase of contact with anger in EFA only applies when you consider the situation to be safe, and the danger of violence nonexistent, either because the logistic set-up prevents it, or because you have made a contract of nonviolence with a person whom you trust. If you are much stronger than the person, you can take your chances on handling any violence that may burst out, although in this case there is a risk that you use EFA techniques to bully the other person into discharging anger that might prevent you from exploiting them.

The second phase of contact, therefore, applies only where it is established that the person needs some help to let out a rage that is a burden or 'consuming.' In such cases the following measures may be used in cases of third party anger:

—If you notice the raised eyebrows and staring eyes of fear, draw the person's attention to this verbally and encourage him or her to frown. Imitate a frown, fix a point on a hard surface, such as a table, and thump it with your fist. Encourage the other person to do the same. Show them how to stick out their lower jaw. Encourage them to breathe out sharply while thumping, and to *look* at the spot they are thumping. Let each thump be for emphasis while having the person describe the situation that makes them angry.

—In an extension of this, give the person a rolled newspaper and encourage them to beat it against a hard object such as the back of a chair. Again, watch for a tendency for the fear expression to supervene and for focus to be lost. Encourage them to frown and *look!* If they are standing, encourage them to keep their feet firmly planted in one spot, with the knees unlocked. (Locked knees may be recognized, even if they are out of sight beneath clothing, by the fact that the person tends to lose balance and topple over while hitting.)

—If the anger is directed toward a particular third party, encourage the person you are helping to choke a towel. The two hands should be touching and twisting in opposite directions. Again, encourage a frown. At the same time, get the person to utter the anger in words. Again, watch for the fear expression, and guide the eyes back into a frowning focus. Many people are frightened by their own anger while choking a towel. Reassure them it is normal. (You will have tested this yourself.) After a while they will most likely throw the towel away across the room in a gesture of dismissal.

—If you notice the person grinding their teeth, ask them to bite on a towel and roar. This may be childish, but it is probably what they need to do and may lead to a substantial relief of tension. It may also make them laugh at themselves, which is hardly unhealthy, and at least means the anger is capable of being dissipated in the face of reality.

—If for one reason or another the anger becomes turned toward you, try to stage a face off, as described in the previous section, in which the ground rule is not moving the feet and not being physically aggressive. Some possible measures to increase conflict safely are:

—Arm wrestling, in the usual way while sitting down at a table, while frowning at each other.

—Facing off, feet fixed, pushing at each other, banging the palms of the hands together, yelling. Again, *focus* on each other's eyes.

—Get the person to push out his or her jaw against your

thumb, while expressing loudly what they are angry about. Maintain a pressure with your thumb, just above the point of the chin, but do not push back strongly. Get *them* to push, to feel their anger lunging forward. (Some people swallow their anger, which involves pulling the jaw back. Pushing against your thumb will mobilize the anger. If the anger is only skin deep, covering hurt or grief, this may make them cry. Then help, as for Grief.)

Anger needs an obstacle. You can be that obstacle, in EFA, without engaging in the battle.

Switching

The tendency to switch from anger to the other emergency reaction, fear, has been mentioned. If the fear expression is merely creeping into a basic expression of rage and lending it a blind, undirected quality, it is best to encourage letting go of it and to fully experience the rage. But if fear seems to be getting the upper hand, and the rage weakening, let it happen (without deliberately frightening the person). Then proceed as in Fear.

Anger and grief may also alternate. Tears of anger are particularly deep if they follow a full expression of rage. The grief may reflect a real hopelessness, and a sadness at the loss of a friendship or difficulties in a relationship. The progression from a 'hard' expression of rage to a 'soft' expression of rage mixed with grief may be very satisfying to the organism—the bitter, hot anger has been flushed out and the crying that follows may be a kind of sad goodbye to unrealistic hope.

On the other hand, a switch from anger or irritation to crying and sobbing *before* the anger has really had a chance to develop, often reflects feelings of impotence and weakness. It is particularly common in women, who in fact experience rage just as powerfully as men but are often trained (one might say 'crushed') into expressing it in the more acceptable (for little girls) form of tears. It is not good EFA to stop a person from crying, but if the angry tears are just beginning, the rage still 'hot,' it may be worthwhile to attempt to re-focus the rage either by making a remark that intensifies it (a reference to some especially annoying detail, perhaps) or by overtly encouraging it: 'But doesn't that make you really mad?' If a man normally capable of expressing rage begins to dissolve into tears of frustration, this may open the way to underlying softness and tenderness and can be encouraged through acceptance socially as dignified tears of mourning or compassion. In general, acceptance must be the key.

Anger may be displaced into nausea and disgust. This may be emotionally valid. (Some very early childhood rage is linked to having to swallow disliked food, or it is part of a damaged oral relationship to the mother.) But if it means the person is incapable of expressing overt rage as an adult, some attempt should be made to allow the rage to surface. Biting a towel in spite of nausea, while making angry sounds, is useful.

It may be worth noting that *hatred,* while not in itself an emotional expression, has more of an active relationship to anger than other 'states' do. Hatred, in contrast to the heat of anger, tends to be cold. Reich remarked describing the emotions of basic contact: 'If you don't love me, I hate you.' Another therapist (Alexander Lowen) has remarked that hatred is 'frozen love,' or love gone cold because of rejection. I would propose that love only turns to hate after another stage has been gone through, that of rage. The cycle seems to be: reaching out with love—rejection by the other person—bitter tears of grief—further rejection of this—an attempt to fight through to the person with burning rage—rejection even of the expression of rage—further rejection of this—a 'freezing' of the rage and grief into cold hatred. More simply: love—rejection—grief—rejection—rage—rejection—hate.

In therapy, we sometimes see this whole cycle being played out, with one emotion succeeding the others as the 'layers' of muscular armor against feeling dissolve. It is useful to be aware of this cycle in EFA, particularly in understanding the process of switching, as well as some problems of resolution.

Resolution

It is possible that after a clear expression of rage a person may be ready to make contact with another person with love and tenderness, but it is not likely. There is often the need for a period of recuperation. The person may feel the need to be alone, do some tidying up or chores, take a walk, or some other neutral activity. This may because the system is still somewhat excited by the flow of adrenaline that the rage has provoked (apparently the composition of the blood remains altered for some hours after the organism has gone into emergency) and the person needs time to be able to feel normally soft and open again. So even if the expression of rage has been complete, do not force contact on the person. Give them time and space. If the person exits with a vigorous slam of the door, don't go after them!

The main problems in resolution are states of depression and guilt. Psychoanalytic theory proposes that depression is rage turned against the self. The rage need not ever have been expressed, it is turning around. The connection between suppressed rage and guilt has also been made by psychoanalysts, but more specifically some of Reich's successors, (e.g. Baker, Konia) propose that guilt after rage occurs when the rage has been only partially expressed, through a process in which the muscles have been activated, but since the action has not been fully carried through, the condition of rage is retained (biochemically or energetically) in the muscle tissue, causing a feeling that is called guilt. (The process may be the same for guilt after any emotional expression: the guilt only occurs if the emotion has been restrained and incomplete.)

Where it seems clear that the expression of anger was half-hearted or cut off abruptly, and it is then followed by depression or guilt, it may be worthwhile trying to reactivate the anger by drawing the person's attention to the anger-producing situation again, and using whatever EFA measures seem appropriate. To stay within the guidelines of noninvasion, this reactivation of the situation should perhaps best be reserved for intimate relationships, where it is justified by the fact that after all you, as the person's friend or partner, have to live with and put up with the intensity of the person's depression or guilt. Reactivation, and the full expression of the rage, may discharge whatever energy has been accumulated and retained.

Problems

Resentment. Nonemergency problems with the expression of anger are usually due to a kind of short-circuiting of the anger process in which rage is deflected into a vicious circle of resentment which drags on and creates resentment or indifference in others, which causes more resentment, and so on. Or else, sarcastic remarks provoke a verbal duel that is as exhausting as any expression of rage, without being satisfying. Or sulking leads to indifference from others and causes a build up of inner pressure. In these processes, pressure is the key word. We acknowledge this in our language, using words such as 'simmering,' or 'his blood is boiling,' or 'he feels like a time bomb waiting to go off.' Just as the pressure in a pressure cooker ultimately depends on the strength of the container's lid, so in the human organism when there is an inner cooking and boiling of resentment, the 'lid' tends to be in the area of the mouth and jaw and back of the neck; the whole area may become stiffer and stiffer as the person holds more and more sensations of resentment that well up from the chest and abdomen, but are held back by the clamped jaw, tight lips, and rigid neck. Eventually an explosion may occur. The person 'blows his stack.' But more often the situation requires the human equivalent of a safety valve, and the person lets off steam in the form of resentful looks or sarcastic remarks. Sarcastic remarks particularly are identifiable as a safety valve function in the fact that they literally tend to emerge from the side of the mouth, through the smallest possible space. One primitive roar of rage or baring of the teeth might release more energy than emerges through a dozen civilized barbed remarks.

Another characteristic of bottled up resentment is 'prickliness.' As Reich pointed out, in the absence of emotional nourishment and support, it is easy to become like a cactus in a desert. Prickliness is often due to feelings of being unloved, but of course—in another vicious circle—prickliness is not necessarily a very lovable trait. It is hard to embrace a cactus.

These are recalcitrant problems—the sarcastic, irritable person is not likely to be provoked into a real, cleansing explosion, since his or her side of the mouth 'digs' are a fairly adequate safety valve. And the prickly person may have lost the capacity to respond to love. These conditions may be worked on in therapy, or in their less severe forms, they may dissolve if the person's life changes in the direction of more love or more satisfying work. But they are outside the scope of EFA which does, after all, work to aid a discharge that is already in process. If they occur in an intimate relationship, an understanding of the underlying rage or need for love may help guide the kind of contact you can make. If you can get the person to really *look* at your eyes, and if you refuse to respond in kind to the digs or wounded prickliness, the contact between you may become intensified to the point where a real rage or a real appeal for love begins to emerge.

Acting out. In rage, acting out takes the form of repeated scenes in which there is a lot of noise or many objects become smashed. A key element is usually the presence somewhere nearby of a third party as an audience, either in the same house, or in the most embarrassing cases in the same public place, such as a restaurant. The scene is most often being staged to cause embarrassment. The fact that this kind of rage is most often associated with women is not biological but another sign of how legitimate rage expression has been so powerfully crushed in many women. When rage is expressed in this way, with the goal of causing embarrassment, enlisting sympathy, or re-awakening love, it is by definition *not rage*. Real rage wants to destroy obstacles to contact, not merely to embarrass another person into behaving differently or to make an appeal for love.

Making a lot of noise and smashing objects at random assure that whatever real rage there is cannot be focused. The choice in EFA is either:

1) to confront the person and focus the apparent rage, using the kind of measures described earlier, or

2) to allow the acting out to run its course without being provoked into joining the battle (essentially a mock battle). To be present and sympathetic to the person afterwards is an attempt to make contact with what the person's real need is.

On the other hand, genuine rage can be dramatic, even melodramatic. If someone at a dinner party gets up and turns over the table, or turns to a neighbor and splashes him or her with the contents of a glass, the eyes may be genuinely blazing with anger. As always, the truth is in the eyes. Focused contact means the rage is genuine. But apart from such observational criteria, genuine rage can be *felt*. Acting out may be brilliant, but it is hollow, carrying no feeling with it for others except embarrassment.

A final word on embarrassment at someone else's rage in a public place, whether genuine or acting out: keep your reaction in proportion. How many times have you been seriously embarrassed in your life? And how many of those times has the scene later become a subject for amused anecdotes? Telling the story will raise a laugh in you and in others. Even though the telling may bring a flush of embarrassment to your face, the incident has probably caused no serious damage to your reputation or self image.

In many people, the fear that is so commonly mixed with anger is a fear of what might happen if their anger is finally let out after years of being held in. This can be a problem. If a person is consistently masochistic, in the sense of turning every angry impulse inward and converting it to an inner suffering, which is in turn used as a weapon and anger substitute in the form of resentment or sulking, any attempt to goad that person into revealing the anger will be very threatening. Normally, your attempt to goad becomes added to the list of the person's grievances and increases the inner tension rather than relieving it. Eventually, you may lose patience and control, make a mistake, and end up feeling you are persecuting an innocent victim. The way out of this is not to goad. If your honest attempt to confront the person's anger through contact and a declaration of where you stand does not get through, leave this problem alone. If it becomes more severe, it may turn into a depression in the person and cause him or her to seek professional help.

Emergency

The main emergency when rage gets out of hand is violence.

Unfortunately, once this point has been reached, there are no specific measures to take except, if you are stronger, to restrain the person, or if you are weaker, to run away or appease. Emotional First Aid can only be effective in the prevention of violence, in defusing it before it starts.

The other side of the same emergency is the threat of suicide, where the person's rage against the world is blocked and turned back against the self. Suicide may be basically, as is well known, 'a call for help.' But it takes energy, and this energy normally contains a large component of anger. The anger tends to be generalized, to be 'against the world' rather than against a specific situation or person, that is, it tends to be unfocused. Emotional First Aid cannot prevent suicide in a person who is seriously disturbed or depressed; anyone with repeated suicidal thoughts would be well advised to seek professional help. EFA can, however, whether working with rage, grief, or fear, prevent an acute situation of emotional distress from overwhelming a person who is otherwise well balanced.

As Crisis Intervention Centers realize, even a voice at the other end of a telephone may prevent some suicides. The crucial element is support, and the fact that the depressed person can discharge pent up emotions, even verbally. Rage is often the main emotion, and should be encouraged to take a focused direction. It should not, however, be unnecessarily exacerbated. Remember that a basic rule for EFA is to prepare a way for the discharge of what is already being expressed, not to encourage the build up of a charge that may be too much for the person to handle.

6

Fear

Fear may range from a low-grade anxiety that is hardly visible externally to a terror that is so dramatic as to be in itself terrifying. As anxiety mounts, some visible signs are a working of the jaw and licking of the lips; yawning in an attempt to compensate for dryness in the mouth (fear inhibits salivation); breaking out into a cold sweat; pallor; and a tendency to tremble. The word 'terror' derives from the same root as 'trembling,' which in extreme fear may overwhelm the entire body. Contraction of the system may be so extreme that the person's hair stands on end (the scalp and other body skin contracts); and circulation may be so withdrawn from the extremities and musculature that the person can no longer remain standing and must collapse. According to Darwin, the eyes and mouth are widely opened and the eyebrows raised; 'the breathing is laboured; the wings of the nostrils are wildly dilated . . . the uncovered and protruding eyeballs are fixed on the object of terror; or they may roll restlessly from side to side.' The pupils of the eyes also become dilated in a reaction that is normally explained as a need to take in every possible detail of the emergency situation. Also, as Darwin noted, the hands and arms spread out rigidly in an expression opposite to the clenching of anger. Darwin's original point that fear and anger were antithetical expressions is supported by the modern evidence, although, as proposed earlier, they have their roots in the same basic emergency reaction.

In the earlier table contrasting fear and anger, fear is seen as a 'charge stroke' in a basic emergency reaction of fear-charge followed by anger-discharge. But anger is not the only discharge; the alternatives are 'fight or flight.' In either case, the muscle system is activated after the initial gasp of fear and moment of wide eyed 'freezing' to take in the situation. The person bursts forward with a lunge of attack, or turns and runs in the opposite direction, chest heaving with panic, eyes darting in all directions to seek out avenues of escape. This can be described as a state of 'hard' flight. But there is another possibility: if protection is at hand in the form of a stronger companion (for example the mother, in the case of a frightened infant), the flight will tend to be soft, a snuggling in for protection, which is followed surprisingly quickly in the case of primates, such as monkeys, by a peeking out toward the danger again in a spirit of curiosity. Even hard flight ends in the same place, if all goes well: a place of protection where the frightened animal or person may get his or her breath back and orient him or herself again with a sense of security. Human mothers who breastfeed their infants even after the first year, when the infant has become mobile, know how the most active and independent child can be instantly reassured after a moment of panic when it rushes to the mother demanding the breast. If the panic has been extreme, the child will burst into tears on arriving at the mother, before snuggling in for comfort. The tears seem to discharge tension.

The process can be summarized:

Stage 1) TERROR ('CHARGE'—gasp of air inward)
Stage 2) SUSPENSION (momentary freezing)
Stage 3) FIGHT (DISCHARGE—breath let out in attack)
or FLIGHT (DISCHARGE—through motor 'hard' flight away, or through soft flight to protection, followed by tears and comfort).

Distress situations occur when the person is stuck in the suspension of stage 2 or in the stage 3 state of hard flight and panic or fight. EFA with fear aims to lead the person toward the state of protection and comfort that, in fact, as a biological organism he or she is seeking. Stage 2, 'suspension,' contains the reactions of both fright rigidity and fright paralysis, as mentioned in Chapter 2. The first condition seems to occur when the organism is 'frozen' but if mobilized would rush to the attack. The hardness of the musculature demonstrates readiness to fight. The second condition is a sign of extreme terror. It is as if the organism can neither run nor fight so it runs *inside*—all sensation is limited to images of flight in the brain. For practical purposes, EFA does not need to distinguish between these states unless the difference is conspicuous. Extremely rigid musculature may show readiness for attack, and there may be other signs of blocked or impending rage. But unless this is very obvious, it is best to treat all immobility as fear.

On a less intense but persistent level, anxiety has its own dynamic. It can start with either anticipated joy or fear—the sensation of excitement, for example before an event that promises to be pleasurable, is an identical sensation in the upper abdomen to the sensation of fear. Both situations of anticipation are mobilizing sensation in the main center of autonomic nervous activity, the solar plexus. Only as the respective situations develop do the sensations develop differently: increasing joy feels clearly different from increasing fear. But in either case, the sensations may run into an emotional block that is anchored in a rigidity of the muscles, which might express movements of joy or fear. Instead of the joy or fear being felt intensely and magnified through spontaneous movement, they again are perceived as anxiety, a feeling of narrowness or choking. This sensation may persist or it may be discharged 'sideways,' as it were, through small-scale harmless actions. An example would be a person excited or fearful before a party, who discharges the anxiety through repeated small adjustments of the clothes or repeated trips to the bathroom.

To sum this up, anxiety develops as follows:

Stage 1)   FEAR or EXCITEMENT (TENSION in area of solar plexus)

Stage 2)   MOVEMENT OF SENSATION AGAINST BLOCK

Stage 3)   PERSISTENT ANXIETY or SUBSTITUTE DISCHARGE.

Experiencing

Simulating fear and terror is harmless for most people, but may be dangerous for some: some of us have experienced severe terror in infancy that has, in the Reichian view, become 'blocked' as a series of muscle tensions affecting the whole body, but most specifically the breathing apparatus and often the muscles of neck, jaw, and eyes. We do not necessarily know if we block in this way, so it is best to be cautious and not exaggerate, and *always* have a friend with you for these simulations, no matter how harmless they seem to be. Once blocked terror is triggered, it is not easy to stop. And do not attempt to imitate 'running panic' if you have any history of high blood pressure or heart problems. If you are going to try these exercises, read the section on fear emergency first, and get your partner to read it too.

1) Stand facing your partner at arm's length. Look him or her in the eye. Make sure both of you are going to stay serious. (There are many temptations to laugh or smile at these 'ridiculous exercises'.) Raise your hands just in front of your shoulders with the palms toward your partner and the fingers splayed open in an expression of 'warding off.' Now simultaneously open your eyes and mouth very wide, being sure to raise the tops of your eyelids high and to raise your eyebrows high as as possible. Now gasp air inward as much as possible, inflating your upper chest to the maximum. Make the gasp *audible.* Hold your breath for a moment with your mouth and eyes still wide open and your upper chest full. Look at your partner's eyes. Then let go of your breath, let your eyes close and your mouth slacken as you let the breath out sharply and fully. Pause an instant, then repeat the procedure. Do not, since there is a danger of hyperventilation, repeat it if you feel dizzy or unsteady on your feet. (If you do feel dizzy, sit down at once.)

Be aware of what you feel in that moment when you have taken in the gasp and you are 'frozen.' Is it the desire to smile (appease)? To hit out? To run away? To scream or yell? Do you 'flash' on any person or situation that has frightened you in the past? Or is the whole exercise dead and mechanical for you? (If so, this is not necessarily a sign that you are beyond fear, but possibly that you tend to block it.) A healthy person will be able to let him or herself feel some real fear in this simulation, without becoming overwhelmed. You may feel quite 'charged' afterward, with tingling sensations, but this will subside. It can, paradoxically, be quite a good experience to go into fear in this way. It is a relief to know that one can feel fear but remain safe, not be carried away.

If you feel comfortable with the first simulation,

2) you can try a version while lying on your back on the floor, knees up and feet flat. Have your partner stand to one side and above you and 'loom' over you. Raise your hands in the warding off gesture, and proceed as in 1). Sigh out a few times afterwards. In this position you may feel more fear. You can accentuate it by pressing your neck and the back of your head against the floor as you gasp in. If you find your legs beginning to shake or tremble, do not worry: this may feel 'insecure,' but letting yourself feel it may, paradoxically, add to your sense of security. (Fear of fear is often worse than fear itself.)

3) In the same position, lying prone on the floor, this time without your partner looming over you, experiment with running panic—start drumming your feet quickly on the floor as if running, pull your shoulders back and press them against the floor as if pushing behind you, push with your hands against the floor, roll your eyes wildly from side to side. *Keep breathing,* noisily if possible, or let out a yell if you feel like it.

Arrange with your partner beforehand to call out for you to stop after about twenty seconds. Don't get completely carried away in this. You may feel some fear, though, enough to understand the expression. You may also feel some relief compared to the previous simulations, since this time your body is in action, you are not remaining in a suspended state but releasing accumulated tension. It is a relief to run.

4) A much milder simulation is simply to see if you can imitate anxiety. Sit down in a chair and remain still. Imagine, perhaps, that you are waiting for an important and somewhat threatening appointment in a place where there is no possibility

of diversion and nowhere to move (let's say a small bare waiting room without magazines where you are left alone). You might start by clenching and unclenching your fists in a restless manner, or fidgeting. Take note of what you tend to do in imitating this anxiety—does your chest stiffen, do you work your jaw, do you hold your legs and buttocks tight, do your eyes become rigid?, and so on.

You might notice in these simulations that there are two main ingredients in a fear situation that is getting worse: first the impossibility of starting to move, second the sense of isolation and of having no one to turn to. EFA for fear must concentrate first on getting the person moving, second on providing contact and comfort.

Distress

Main distress signs for fear can be summarized:

A) General signs:

—difficulty in breathing (uneven heaving of the chest or unusual tightness in a person whom you know normally breathes more freely).

—increasing pallor of the skin, possibly accompanied by visible breaking out in beads of sweat.

—increasing fidgetiness or agitation.

—signs of dryness in the mouth and throat—working of the jaw, frequent swallowing, licking of the lips; increasing dryness of the voice, tendency to speak in a croak or more huskily and lower than usual.

—increased blinking (may represent an attempt to restore moisture to eyeballs that are becoming dry through activation of the emergency branch of the autonomic nervous system); or conversely, increased protrusion of the eyeballs and the development of a fixed stare.

—clamping together of the knees tightly.

—shakiness or trembling (in itself not necessarily fear, since it may indicate anxious excitement or anticipation).

B) 'Freezing':

—rigid immobility of the whole body.

—rigid immobility of the eyes, which protrude and stare blankly into space.

—jaw hangs open.

—breathing apparently suspended (only slight movement around the area of the waist).

—inability to speak, 'struck dumb'.

C) Panic:

—frantic rolling of the eyes with desperate or piteous expression.

—mouth open with corners turned down as in the grief expression, but with a tendency for the neck muscles to be contracted and stand out in cords (this represents a suppressed scream).

—agitated rushing about, bumping into things, repeating actions compulsively and irrationally (e.g. getting a tissue, wiping nose, throwing tissue away, then repeating the whole sequence; or lighting a cigarette then stubbing it out, i.e. agitation without contact).

—extreme shakiness and shuddering of the body.

—constant repetition of a word or phrase.

—splaying wide of the fingers and/or compulsive jerking of the hands.

—self-destructive behavior, such as banging into walls (this seems to represent a blind flight away).

—desperate and convulsive clinging to someone else (flight towards).

—hyperventilation (uncontrollable panting); see section *EMERGENCY*.

Provocation

It is not necessary to discuss the obvious ways of frightening a person, such as bullying, threatening violence, or pushing them into danger. Some more subtle ways may be worth mentioning.

Destructive threats may provoke anger as well as fear, or even rational withdrawal. The kind of threat that seems most likely to provoke fear alone is the threat of withdrawal of support that is normally given. If a person has been relying on you for some kind of support, and you are now withdrawing it, never underestimate the fear this may provoke. Support in the literal sense of keeping another organism from falling is the most basic primal antidote to fear, since there is evidence that the most primitive fears in newborn infants and primates are those linked with 'falling anxiety'—being dropped by or losing the grip on the mother. At this primitive level, which therapeutic evidence suggests lives on in us all, support equals mother. Likewise, withdrawal of support equals withdrawal of mother. Even if the support has been metaphorical or symbolic, far removed from actual physical support (examples are financial support, support for advice seeking), its withdrawal may be met with panic, especially in a person who has difficulties being independent. An emotionally self-supporting person for whom support is a welcome help but not a perpetual necessity, does not have this difficulty. So even if you withdraw support from someone and the first reaction you receive is rage, do not underestimate the fear content.

There are also many subtle and indirect ways of threatening a person that are nevertheless extremely potent because they evoke childhood fears. An adult's looming above a child is one of the most potent triggers of fear. Even among adults, if one insists on always looming or towering above another, sitting always higher, looking intimidatingly downward, the result will be the evocation of at least a continual low grade anxiety. Watch your habits in this way; many tall people in particular feel insecure and awkward because of their height, on the one hand, but compensate by crowding in on shorter people, on the other. Or, if you set out to comfort someone by sitting on the arm of their chair and towering over them as you reassure them, do not be surprised if your reassurances are not well received.

Similarly, in comforting a person who is frightened, it does not make much sense to sweep them off their feet and smother them in your arms in a vigorous movement. No matter what trust they already have in you, your behavior is, at a biological level, threatening. There is a fine line between smothering and protection.

Finally, as is well known, panic is infectious. This seems to be true much more than of anger. Although the situation is commonplace of a crowd dispersing in panic and becoming a stampeding mob, the opposite situation of a crowd becoming whipped up into a frenzy of murderous rage, as in a lynch mob, seems to require more effort by a leader to induce. Fear, in the form of constant anxiety, seems to be nearer the surface in most people than any other emotion. In a crowd, where tension is high and contact relentless, it may only take one person's explosion into panic to trigger the whole group into flight, as in a flock of birds wheeling away with a single bird who takes off in a hurry. But even in a room with two people, increasing anxiety in one will tend to trigger the same in the other even if it is at first responded to with irritation. Think which situation makes you most quickly upset: if you are with a friend and he or she gets suddenly worked up with rage and starts sounding off about something, or if you are with another friend who suddenly becomes acutely anxious and almost hysterical about some impending event. Which would tend to come quicker, your anger in the first situation or your anxiety in the second?

Your own anxiety can provoke anxiety in others. This is not to say that your anxiety can be eliminated on the spot in the service of Emotional First Aid. Rather, if you are seriously anxious, and on the way to becoming frightened by a situation, this is no time for you to administer EFA. (The slight anxiety that is felt as part of anticipation or excitement, when your energy is mobilized for action but you have not yet begun to act, is normal and not infectious.)

Contact (1): Words

The only words that have any effect in the EFA of fear are those that draw the person into contact. Anything else in the way of reassurances about a situation will be useless if a person is frozen or in panic. As is acknowledged in the common phrase, 'my reassurances fell on deaf ears,' the main problem to deal with in fear is that the person is cut off from contact with you either by the wall of his or her frozen paralysis or by the confusion of flight and panic. This is visible as a temporary 'contact block' at the level of the eyes, which are either rigidly 'unseeing' or so mobile with panic that perception is confused. To the eyes of the frightened person you either do not exist (the only images in front of them are from their own brain) or you exist in the form of monstrous and often threateningly fragmented distortions. In view of this, whatever words you use must reduce ultimately to one word—*look*. It can be 'look at me,' 'look at my eyes,' 'look at what's happening,' look at this or look at that, but always look. Get the person's eyes directed outwards, get them steady, in focus, preferably on your own eyes. Since you cannot manipulate the eyes physically, words must suffice for this, but you can reinforce the words with gestures.

Reassurance is not very effective in cases of low-grade anxiety, which tends to cause the same dulling or confusion of visual perceptions as fear, although on a lesser level. According to much physiological evidence, the eyes function largely as a sort of outer layer of the brain: they are not only windows into the brain, but they reflect deep levels of brain functioning and even perform some outer level brain functions in processing information. This means that a noticeable suspension or confusion of perception through the eyes, in the form of immobility or hypermobility, is actually a reflection of what is happening in the brain. To reduce some complex physiological data to a simple rule of thumb: if you cannot make contact with a person's eyes, you will not be able to make contact with their brain. In this sense your verbal reassurances do not only fall on deaf ears, your physical gestures or expressions of support are seen with blind eyes.

Since fear has this paralyzing effect on the more sophisticated levels of brain functioning, visual processing, etc., as well as progressively even on less sophisticated functions such as keeping balance and maintaining an upright position, it is as well to realize that EFA with a frightened person must, and only can, make contact at a primitive level. For a brief moment of time, at least, the person has become something like a baby.

Anxiety. Perhaps the most useful verbal suggestion you can make to someone who is in a severe state of anxiety that threatens their functioning is that they stick one finger down their throat and induce the gag reflex. This may seem a bizarre remedy, but is an old standby of actors with stage fright or people with interview fright, who feel so anxious that they are almost choking, as if words will never be able to come. Gagging in this way is physiologically inducing the first stage of vomiting, but unless you really do have an irritated stomach, it is unlikely that you will actually vomit. Your throat muscles, chest wall, and diaphragm will however contract abruptly. This does not have an emotional effect and will not aid understanding, but it 'short circuits' the anxiety, by mechanically opening the breathing passage (which anxiety has made tight and narrow) and temporarily breaking whatever tension has built up in the chest muscles through anxious breath holding. Gagging may also release any mask-like rigidity that has been creeping over the face. And it gets the person breathing more openly, making him or her more ready for action. It is not a pleasant experience, since it goes against the usual direction of flow in your digestive tube, but with a little practice it can become not really unpleasant, and the benefits in relief of anxiety far outweigh a moment's unpleasantness. ('A little practice' might be to try gagging before breakfast in the morning. It is not necessary to make a ritual of this, once you are comfortable with the knowledge that you can gag easily whenever you want.)

Anxiety may be suppressing pleasure and excitement. Take the example of a woman who is preparing for a huge party. Her anxiety is causing her to rush around repeating various actions compulsively, taking things out of the oven, putting them back in, and so on. If she runs out of compulsive actions to perform, her anxiety becomes her real distress. But it would be quite inappropriate to attempt the EFA of fear. Instead, encourage her to identify her underlying feeling. The odds are it will be simple excitement. Under the circumstances, the best thing is to suggest diversion of the energy into some other activity that is less compulsive, for example, that she and you take a walk before the party. Another example is the well known pre-exam anxiety suffered by students. This is not all fear. Much of it is excitement, a feeling of bursting with information and ideas. It does no harm to acknowledge this, and then undertake some unrelated activity that calms and diverts the person during the period of waiting. The ideas will burst to the surface the moment the exam begins and they are needed.

Freezing. Freezing most often occurs after a severe shock; such as an automobile accident. In such cases it is functional; it is of help to the organism *not* to react. People often report that in crisis circumstances, they have behaved not only calmly but 'almost like a machine,' or 'somehow they knew what to do.' The problem here is not that the person has become frozen in this functional way, but that as the frozen state thaws out, all the emotions of terror that have been suspended during the crisis flood to the surface. In some cases, it is weeks later when the nightmares and trembling start.

There are two options for EFA in such cases. The first is to attempt gently to thaw out the frozen state in a situation where you know the person is secure. (For example, if acute terror is to be experienced, it may as well be when there is a friend to help, not later when everyone has abandoned the scene and assumed the suffering person is back to normal.) The second is to wait for the person to unfreeze spontaneously and deal with whatever fears or terrors emerge piece by piece. There is something to be said for this second approach, since it is consistent with self regulation of the organism. In the final analysis, many oranisms seem to know what is good for them. On the other hand, without pushing, when you are at hand to help it does make sense to try to provoke a sudden thaw of the frozen state, provided you do so gently and desist if such gentle efforts do not work. Too often a person will remain frozen for a long time, thaw suddenly when there is no one available for contact, and end up in a hospital under sedation or wondering if they are going insane, since the later surges of terror are disconnected by intervening time from the original emergency and tend to contain images and material from childhood.

Panic. This cannot be dealt with by merely verbal means—your words will not get through.

Contact 2: Touching

Anxiety. Although verbal reassurance alone is of doubtful value, we instinctively know that, if accompanied by gentle physical contact, it can come through to the person. Most of us are comfortable with taking an anxious person under our wing for a moment by putting our arm on their shoulder and squeezing them gently while uttering some words of reassurance. We then let go, having given them some of our energy, as it were, for the challenge in front of them. This process of gentle physical reassurance (the word 'reassurance' implies a regaining of a sense of physical 'sureness' that we can provide), alternating with letting go, seems to be more effective, perhaps because it respects a basic pulsation in human activity, than a physical touch which is unremitting. We have all probably had the experience of being physically comforted by a person for just a little too long. If the helping hand lingers, if the supportive embrace seems to cling to us, we may feel manipulated or confused: the protector may be out to get us after all, or is it in fact the protector who is frightened?

In other words, stay sensitive to your own feelings. If protecting a person by touching them is comforting *you,* do not fool yourself that you are helping. Rather, you are both doing the perfectly normal thing (although it is not EFA) of clinging to each other for protection. Similarly, if you offer support by literally holding someone up, stop it if you realize you are leaning on *them.*

Freezing. The challenge here is to try to jolt the person out of their frozen state without giving them a shock. If a few simple ways of triggering contact do not work, it is best not to push the situation, and to opt for standard methods of treatment such as providing warmth and rest. You might also, after a severe emergency such as an accident that has shocked the person without injuring them, try to make sure that there is the possibility of contact and comfort at hand for the person for some days ahead. The trouble is that the longer the person stays out of contact and copes mechanically with the aftermath of the crisis, the more intense the eventual thawing out may be (more like an overwhelming spring flood). Some simple ways of making contact and provoking a thaw are:

—Take the person's hand, look gently into their eyes and ask them to look at you. It may help to massage the hand gently, particularly the wrists. If looking provokes sobbing, you can proceed as for 'grief.'

—If you are already intimate with the person, take them in your arms, from the side, not smotheringly, 'under your wing,' embrace them firmly for a few moments, then ask them to look at you.

—Put your hands on the person's cheeks and ask them to look at you, turning their head gently toward you. (Be aware that touching a frightened person on the head or face may trigger an outburst of terror or anger.)

—If the person remains out of contact, encourage them to lie down in a fetal position. Make sure their body is folded forward with the knees up. Wait quietly with your hand touching them on the back of the neck. If intimate with them, you might try stroking their hair or gently massaging the scalp. (One of the main elements of freezing with fear is contraction of the scalp muscle; it is as if the whole upper head freezes.)

—If the person is lying down and still seems very stiff, rock his or her body gently with your hand on the shoulder, shaking it slightly. This may induce trembling, which you can encourage verbally.

—Ask the person to open the eyes very wide and look at you. Make sure they also raise their eyebrows in the basic fear expression. Ask them to breath *in*. If they hold their breath, make sure they breathe out. This may mobilize the fear.

Be prepared for any event or emotion as the person thaws out, and *accept it,* even if it is irrational rage turned against you or anyone else in the environment. Also accept your own fear. You are not superhuman, and as stated earlier, fear is infectious. In particular, if you are normally made anxious by trembling in your own body, you may be made anxious by the other person trembling. But let it happen. Do not try to brace the person against you: the more rigid the person remains, the more the fear will 'back up' to emerge later in a distorted form (such as nightmares or irrational outbursts at inappropriate moments). Trembling and shaking discharge accumulated tension.

Panic. Again there are two approaches. First, allow panic and agitation to develop fully while protecting the person against injury. Second, 'steady' the person and bring them back into contact and subsequent comfort. This is a matter of timing, since the second option is in fact a way of protecting the person against injury. It is probably a good thing to give the panicking person some elbow room so that accumulated tension can be discharged through motor activity. The second phase, steadying, should ideally only apply when the person is already on the way back to contact and is calming down, a process that you can encourage once it is underway. However, in practice, it may be necessary for safety's sake to steady a person somewhat earlier than is biologically good for them. It is important to *accept* panic as a necessary functional discharge. Too often onlookers rush to restrain a panicking person because the extreme mobility of panic provokes great anxiety in those who normally keep their own panic 'frozen.' A literal or chemical straitjacket is normally applied not to protect the panicking person but to protect other people from all that emotion.

It is best here to start with a few don'ts:

—Do *not* stop a person from screaming, whether after an accident or in a personal crisis. Screaming is probably the best thing 'energetically' for the person, and if allowed to run its course, is almost a guarantee that the main content of the terror will not return in waking or sleeping nightmares. Too often people are restrained from screaming and left to deal with waking up in the middle of the night *wanting* to scream. If in reading this you find the idea of screaming makes you anxious, take a safe time and place and practice screaming for yourself; open your mouth wide in a big 'square' shape with the muscles of your neck contracted, close your eyes tightly, and scream with a *high pitched* 'AAAA' sound (as in the word 'man') which feels as if it is vibrating out of your *head*. (From your chest it is more likely to be an angry yell.)

—On the other hand, do *not* induce screaming in a person who is not already screaming. The previous instruction (contact

1) to 'make a sound' may induce screaming, but do not try any further measures. (Some measures, which you may have heard of from therapy, involve manipulations of the neck and jaw that are best left to experts and even then must be used carefully.)

—Do *not* restrain the person from trembling or fidgeting or moving about, unless the movement will cause them physical harm.

Some EFA measures:

—For hyperventilation, i.e. uncontrolled panicky pumping and panting of the chest accompanied by an increasing lack of contact, proceed as outlined in *Emergency*.

—Constantly urge the person to get the breathing down from the chest mainly into the abdomen, to *'Breathe low and slow.'*

—Deal with violent panicky attacks on you or anyone else by restraining the person and at the same time insisting loudly and repetitively that they *look at your eyes.*

—If possible, deal with self-destructive behavior, such as head banging, by putting padding between the head and any hard surface. If this is not possible, restrain the person in your arms but *leave them room to struggle* and discharge tension.

—If the person is calming down from motor activity, but the eyes are still rolling around in panic and distress is severe, take them firmly by the shoulders, give them a firm jolt, and encourage them to look at you. Ask them to open their eyes and look at your eyes. This may induce sobbing and consequent relief.

Switching

Switching from an expression of fear is normally into anger or grief. (Hysterical laughter is obviously far from being an excape into joy, and can be treated like panic, by steadying and focusing contact.) As with all switching, once a tendency toward a new emotion is strongly established, this should be accepted. EFA is not concerned with making judgements as to whether an expression is appropriate.

Some minor signs of anger building up are tearing and twisting at clothes or objects, grinding the teeth, and holding the breath in an inflated position. Watch for an explosion. Remember that anger is most dangerous when mingled with fear. Unfortunately, you have little option but to allow the anger to emerge and then attempt to deal with it as outlined in Chapter 5. The opposite route, of trying to pressure the person further into their fear to cover the anger, is a dangerous maneuver since it will be experienced as an attack.

Some signs of grief are wringing of the hands, clutching at the head or face, and rocking movements of the body. The person needs to be held. If your level of intimacy permits this, it will channel the fear into a softer expression of crying, which will in time discharge it. If physical contact would be too invasive, proceed as outlined in Chapter 4. A deep discharge of grief at whatever has happened, and contact with a source of reassurance, which tends to produce crying with relief and gratitude, is a natural and perhaps essential phase in the resolution of fear.

Panic may contain switching as a main element, and when a person is alternating rapidly between outbursts of sobbing, spasms of terror, and lunges of anger and aggression, Emotional First Aid is not easy. But contact, if gently insistent, should steady the person into whichever of these emotions needs most powerfully to be expressed, or at least slow down the process of switching to a manageable rate.

Resolution

If in extreme fear the person is reduced by feelings of panic and vulnerability to a state of being like a baby, resolution consists of a beginning to emerge from this state after the period of support and comfort that the EFA should have provided. So, once the person has calmed down, it is as well to encourage movements toward reestablishing a more adult position, such as a wish to stand up and move around, or to discuss the fearful situation rationally. Even jokes about it help reestablish confidence: if the person makes a joke *after* having fully experienced fear or grief, this cannot be called an attempt at escape from the feeling.

The problem in resolution after fear is similar to that after grief, a question of timing—when to accept the person's struggles to return to a 'normal' attitude and behavior, and when to discourage them for the time being so as to make sure the emotional discharge really is complete. Fear adds the problem that, more than in all but the most severe cases of grief, the organism has been severely shaken and the tendency to relapse into a need for help is strong. Even physiologically it takes time for the body to adjust. You can help the adjustment by remaining calm, steady, and supportive. This will enable the person's autonomic nervous system to reestablish a balance after being flooded with chemicals associated with emergency.

As with severe grief, the person who has experienced severe terror needs to be assured of a support system afterwards. This need may lead to a clinging to the source of help for some while after this is really necessary. In general, the suggestions made in the section on resolution after grief apply equally after fear.

Problems

As with grief and rage, where intermediate states of depression or resentment present more problems than any temporary block of the expression once it is underway, so with fear the most persistent problem is low-grade anxiety. It is as if fear is ever present but not mobilized. The person, whether semifrozen or constantly agitated, seems to exert a drain on other people. With anxiety the situation is made even worse by the characteristic perceptual blocking associated with fear: the person cannot see reason, cannot hear reassurance. You cannot get through.

An associated problem is that very basic fears are so threatening to the organism that even their perception is blocked, but the condition of contraction of the organism remains. Just as specific anger may be repressed and displaced into generalised resentment or petty irritation, a basic fear may become displaced into an anxiety about something seemingly nonthreatening or irrelevant. The case histories of psychoanalysis abound with examples of irrational phobias—a fear of spiders when perhaps the person is afraid of being touched (touching has been a threat since long ago); of water when the person is perhaps afraid of being overwhelmed by longing (longing would excite the person to breath more deeply, but this is suppressed with a suffocated sensation like drowning); of going out into crowds when the person is repressing a deep anger against other people, and so on. In such cases, there are no proper equivalents. One person's phobia of spiders may have a different associational meaning from someone else's.

Some forms of therapy attempt to tackle such phobias directly, as does behavioral therapy, which seeks to decondition the person from the phobia. But new phobias or distorted versions of the old tend to emerge. A therapy that attempts to take the energetic dynamics of the whole organism into account, such as Reichian therapy or psychoanalysis in the hands of some practitioners, would postulate that only when the underlying condition of fear is removed will the tendency to form phobias disappear. This usually means long term therapeutic work. But how can the ordinary person, or the EFA helper, react to such a phobia? If another person shows a constant fear of spiders, for example, and insists on turning the whole environment upside down in attempts to keep it spider-free, our instinctive reaction may well be annoyance rather than the wish to help, even when asked. It must be admitted that when a person who is apparently functional, in the sense that they are not under treatment for illness, displays a persistent phobia, this creates a net result of antagonism in others, as effectively as does the complaining masochist. Fear, like grieving pain, can have the result of provocation. If you react with honest anger at such provocation, you have fallen into the trap of becoming a persecutor or an enemy to someone who is genuinely frightened— but of something else, nothing you can reach. Apart from gently steering the person with a phobia toward professional help, the only course is patience. But beware of becoming the victim of the other person's phobias: do not let *your* life be influenced by the need to ensure total protection against spiders.

Sometimes a deep anxiety is not channeled into a specific phobia but is instead 'free floating,' available to attach itself to any event or object. Here again, other people may find themselves being drawn into unexpected reactions of anger. Remember the possibility that such anger in you may be partly a cover-up for your own fear, which occurs as you are 'infected' by the other person's. Free-floating anxiety seems particularly infectious, precisely because it lacks an identified object. If you pick it up you tend to attach it to your own fears. For example, a friend's anxiety that seems objectless, but which is perhaps connected with some life situation such as a bad marriage, may make you anxious about something more relevant to you, such as an upcoming journey.

In such situations, you may certainly either offer your help and reassurance or encourage the person to seek professional help. But at the same time, just as when you are required to care for extreme and longterm situations of grief, you do have the right to protect yourself. Self protection against the harmful effects of another person's emotional trouble is not inconsistent with EFA. On the contrary, any effective helper must take necessary steps to protect him or herself against infection that would decrease effectiveness. After all, we think nothing of it when a medical helper in an epidemic wears a mask for protection. And we are certainly grateful that our surgeons keep their instruments sterile. In Emotional First Aid, your perceptions are like the instruments of a surgeon. As Reich emphasized, they must be kept clean. This does not mean that you become detached, any more than the surgeon keeps his instruments clean by not touching the patient's wound. But you have the right to keep a balance between involvement and detachment, to retain your own freedom of emotional movement.

Chronic emergency patterns. The main problems in EFA of fear can be traced to the chronic emergency patterns mentioned earlier (Chapter 2). These patterns, varying according to the person's character structure, are activated in any situation of emotional distress, but never more clearly than in fear. It can be said that the fear of fear underlies *all* emotional distress inasmuch as blocked grief and blocked rage are ultimately due to the fear of letting go and perhaps being deeply frightened. Many people react to the least anxiety in a predictable way. Without exploring what I have called the ambivalent emergency reactions, which underlie the complexities of masochistic provocation, it is worth mentioning here the basic reactions of freezing, collapse, clinging, panic, and attack. This chapter has already discussed freezing and panic. The other three reactions present specific problems.

Collapse. This is similar to freezing, where the person's 'ice' can be either broken through movement or thawed through contact. The difference is that instead of a rigid frozen state, this is a soft, flaccid paralysis where the skin is cool and the muscles have no tension. As already mentioned, the same rules apply as with freezing: initiate contact and movement. But such measures, in collapse, may have to be more long term. It is as if the energy, rather than being frozen at the surface like ice on a pond, has retreated to some dark and cold spot in the depths of the organism. It takes much longer for warmth to reach it, and there are no torrents of panic on thawing out, but rather a gradual coming back to life. When infant-like needs to be cradled or rocked emerge, this is a good sign. Recovery is gentle.

Clinging. This may take the form of actual physical clinging or of a kind of smothering of the prospective helper with detail and complaint. Although the person means no harm, the net result is to infect the helper with the fear and to produce further reactions of anger as the helper tries to struggle free. Approach toward contact with the helper is of course much to be desired in EFA. This becomes clinging when the contact is not followed by a natural withdrawal in which the person returns to adult, independent state. The clinging person begins to almost feed off the helper. As the helper, your support becomes a drain on you, but if you withdraw it, the result is anxiety. This is, however, the only solution. If you have done your best, the person's chronic anxiety is too much for EFA to help, and you must urge them to seek help elsewhere with a professional who has experience in weaning a person from this sort of over-attachment.

Attack. Some people react to any emergency situation with anger and verbal attack. Watch, however, for the give-away expression of fear in the forehead and eyes. You may point it out. But this may be the excuse for further attack. In its most extreme form, this chronic emergency reaction can be paranoia. But a great many rather lively people show it. It is, after all, a vigorous and often functional reaction to emergency. The problem is that it is a denial of the softer emotions of grief and of vulnerability. The person suffers from this hardening. The only solution is for you to avoid any kind of hard reaction in yourself, since the opposition of two hard reactions becomes easily a battle: steel is met with steel. It may be a test of your pride in your own strength, but it is useful to give, and to remain soft. Remember, you see that fear in the eyes. Speak to it, reassure it. Do not threaten. The person may feel safe with you and become able to soften and let some of the fear in. (Of course, the situation is different when you see the concentrated frown of anger in forehead and eyes, in which case your softness may indeed be appeasement.)

If a person shows a consistent pattern of emergency behavior that forms a wall against all your efforts to reach through, you may have to accept that this is more than an EFA problem.

Emergency

Self-destructive behavior in agitation has already been discussed under grief. The main specific emergency for fear is *hyperventilation.*

Hyperventilation may be puzzling to those who have never seen it. A person will sometimes hyperventilate under the pressure of a severe emergency. The signs are:

—Quick, panting breathing that continues without stopping even if the person is urged to slow down. This is *high* breathing, i.e. the chest heaves up and down.

—Indications of what is medically called 'tetany': progressive rigidification of the upper body, tightening around the mouth, and contraction of the hands. This last is specifically recognizable as a rigidification of the fingers and a drawing of the thumbs across the palm. The hands thus become locked.

—At the same time the person is out of eye contact even if the eyes are open, and it is seemingly impossible to make contact.

The whole picture is of progressive freezing and locking of the body musculature, in the presence of continued fast breathing. This can be a dangerous condition, since the blood supply to the brain is affected by increasing alkalinization, and the person may eventually black out. Ways of treating it are as follows:

—A traditional first aid method is to take a paper bag and ask the person to breathe into it for a while, thus forcing a rebreathing of air, which eventually restores the chemical balance in the tissues.

—A more simple method (especially if there are no paper bags available), although it requires more contact, is to block the person's breathing by putting your hand over the mouth and nose and pressing firmly in such a way as to block all air intake. Count to twenty, unless the person squirms to push you away (in which case the hyperventilation is not severe since he or she is relatively mobile). Under the circumstances, you will not suffocate the person. (Pearl divers hyperventilate deliberately to a partial extent so as to be able to suspend breathing for long periods.) Withdraw your hand and encourage contact, telling the person to look at your eyes and to breathe *slowly*. If this does not work, block the breathing again.

—You may try to stop hyperventilation by verbal means alone, encouraging contact and slower breathing, but if these do not work, you have to take further steps, as above.

What the person is feeling is usually increasing paralysis, a sense of being spaced out and detached, and increasing sensations of sharp currents like pins and needles in face, arms, and legs. It is as if the fear situation is so overwhelming that the organism becomes stuck in the normal emergency reaction of a startled intake of breath. The intake keeps repeating itself. The person becomes 'pumped up,' as it were, and is unable to discharge through emotional expression.

Some people have a chronic problem of hyperventilation in even minor emergency states, or from generalized anxiety. They should be referred to professional help. But any person who tends to block the emotions of fear, or who is subjected to a sudden shock, may go into a state of hyperventilation. If measures are taken as above, it soon passes, and there is nothing to be alarmed about.

After you have helped a person deal with the hyperventilation, and the breathing has returned to normal, stay with them for a while, since either one of two things may happen: the person may suddenly enter into contact again with a memory of the emergency situation that has provoked the hyperventilation, and it may start again, or else after a pause of some minutes there may be a strong tendency toward an emotional discharge either of fear or grief. Watch for the signs of this impending discharge (preliminary signs of terror or crying) and encourage them gently, remembering that this is often an area of emotional expression which is in itself frightening to the person. Another possibility is that the person is frightened to express the emotion in front of you. Make it clear that you're there for support.

7

Joy

Expression

Joy is antigravity. It leaps upward and outward. Children and animals jump and bounce for joy. Adults feel 'high.' In fact, our center of gravity becomes higher; in joy our chests fill, our shoulders expand, and we become taller. Our step becomes springy. Our features are drawn upwards. As Darwin pointed out, a smile lifts the corners of the mouth, the upper cheeks become raised.

Our voices in speech contain higher frequencies when we are joyful, and although we cannot distinguish these frequencies separately, we sense them. Music expresses this in terms of pitch—in Beethoven's Ode to Joy, the voices rise higher and higher like steps of sound. Joy is soft expansion. Our skin becomes warm and pink. It 'glows.' Our eyes sparkle. Joy is also light. Glowing light and antigravity light.

It is at the top of a scale of steps. At the bottom is depression. Down, not high. Cold, not warm, low frequencies in the voice, not high. Lustreless, not light. Depression is gravity.

There seems to be a whole series of steps between joy and depression:

Joy
Rejection
Rage
Hate

Grief

Detachment

Depression.

Perhaps the sequence varies, but the key step is the one just below joy: rejection. We reach out in joy and are blocked by a wall in someone else. From then on it may be a tumble down the steps, part or all the way down.

Joy seems to be the emotion evoked by contact itself. It is impossible to imagine joy with a sense of isolation, unlike grief, anger, and fear. A person can, of course, be alone with joy, but there is always contact with something, if not another human being, nature itself. Even in the sight of the first flower of spring or of the ocean for the first time after a long stay inland, joy is at least doubled if shared. The sharing does not have to be with words. There is often silent sharing with joy, as if contact between organisms is occurring at levels almost of the plasma in the tissues.

Experience

How accessible is joy in you? If you stand up, shift your weight to the balls of your feet, spring slightly on your heels, let yourself smile, and draw in a gentle deep breath to your chest, do your eyes begin to look around for something to enjoy? Or is this simply embarrassing? It is hard to simulate joy, perhaps because it requires contact. Perhaps a memory will help. Often a memory of the first time you did or saw something that turned out to be special. First meetings, first expansions in a new way, seem to leave us changed inside. There has often been an element of wonder, what Wordsworth called 'surprised by joy.' It is difficult to simulate joy 'cold,' but easier if you begin by simulating wonder: let your eyes and mouth open wide and take a soft breath into your chest. Imagine perhaps a child seeing a birthday cake brought into the room. The natural follow up in breathing out is a sigh of 'Ah!,' which tends to leave the face in the joy expression: an open smile with the corners of the mouth turned up, the cheeks pressing upward to crinkle the corners of the eyes.

But in imitating the first stage of joy, the expression of wonder, you may become aware that it is not unlike the expression of fear: both are an opening of the mouth and eyes as if to take in the maximum impression from the environment. Only the pace and the feeling are different: wonder is soft where fear is hard, and the expansion of the chest is steady, not abrupt. When wonder is sudden enough to be surprise, it becomes very like the startle reflex of fear.

It may be useful to imitate various degrees of surprise, ranging from gentle wonder through abrupt fear. The taking in aspect of both joy and fear, or in energy terms the apparent fact that both are preceded by a charging of the organism with excitement and impression, means that if a person has become blocked against the expression and experiencing of fear, the capacity for joy has also become blocked. The price for all emotional blocking is a progressive immobilization of parts of the organism. Joy, which is mobile, reaching, and expansive if allowed to let go, becomes trapped inside the armor of pain.

Distress

In the cases previously discussed, distress has consisted of the emotion pressing for release and being held in. When joy presses for release, it may also be held in, but since the sensation of joy rising in the organism is pleasurable, distress is perceived less acutely. Rather, the person deadens him or herself slightly. This deadening may be seen by the person as self-control, modesty, politeness, or moral behavior. It often forms a wall of self-satisfaction. The person's self image is involved. For this reason, although Emotional First Aid for blocked joy can consist only of a few simple measures to open the way for its sharing, even simple measures of contact can be seen as threatening.

Why does the capacity for joy become deadened? Surely it is by definition pleasurable, and human beings naturally seek pleasure. The answer must be that, when the pleasure of joy moves the organism, it is experienced as anxiety, not pleasure. It has already been mentioned how the first sensations of excitement and of anxiety are a similar tension in the upper abdomen.

When excitement presses against a block, it becomes anxiety.

Restraint has its place. Many of us have had the experience of learning good news and restraining our joyful reaction until we can share it with a particular person whom we love. We know this sharing will be more intense than if we spill out our joy to the first bystander we meet. Such restraint can be seen as part of the energy economy of a healthy organism. But in our society, restraint has become pervasive except for special occasions. We need *permission* to express joy, and this is given by certain social situations that institutionalize it: we are allowed to express joy when we have drunk too much alcohol and are 'high,' or when our home team has won a game. These occasions permit us to slap each other's backs, hug each other, or jump up and down exuberantly. This institutionalization of joy seems to ensure that we experience it in a safe context and, most important, in a situation where other people are permitted, even socially required, to be joyful too.

In the presence of our own blocked joy, the sight of another person's joy produces in us unbearable pain. We may feel empty, hostile, conscious of our own deadness or despair. The next section of this chapter, on provocation, discusses the important social phenomenon of envy. One of the main causes of the suppression of joy is envy avoidance.

The most usual sign of distress in blocking joy is embarrassment. It may be hard to even talk or write about joy. When I wrote the beginning of this chapter, an internal censor told me it was 'too corny.' I have to get through my own embarrassment to let it stand. Public embarrassment causes blushing and the avoidance of eye contact. Physiologically, the organism has expanded with pleasure, and contact with another organism might lead to movements or actions or avowals of feeling that are not socially permissible. The elaborate social mechanisms of the repression of joy indicate first that this soft expansion of feeling is acknowledged to be extremely powerful, and second that it is perceived as dangerous.

The roots of this danger seem to be in the very capacity of joy to overwhelm self control and urge the organism toward contact, especially sexual contact. We know this from adult experience. Joy can be more infectious than fear. People get high at parties and may become involved in rash sexual adventures. (Afterwards, they have the excuse that they were drunk, which serves to integrate the experience into normal life: alcohol and drugs have formed part of the institutional joy of many societies apparently for this reason.) At victory celebrations after the end of a war or the liberation of a country, complete strangers end up making love. At times people do genuinely foolish things that they regret. A perpetual, unrestrained permission to 'enjoy' would, in most societies, lead not to freedom of emotional and sexual expression, but to license and abuse. This may be regrettable, but has to be acknowledged. Writers such as Reich and the educator A. S. Neill have discussed the fact that a healthy adult or child functions in a self-regulating manner that is instinctively 'moral' in the sense that it does not abuse the rights of others (a sensitive person respects the rights of others because of a capacity to identify with them), but that in most societies the repression of pleasure in children has led to the accumulation of destructive emotions that genuinely have to be restrained. As the saying goes, 'freedom cannot come overnight.'

Embarrassment has a sexual content, fear of exposure of what we really want. It is as if in exposing our joy, we expose our sexuality. If you doubt this, think of one of the most potent reasons for the suppression in children of the natural desire to share and express pleasure with strangers. We tell our children not to talk to strangers because we know there are too many strangers who will abuse or molest our children. We encourage our children to be mistrustful. Rightly so. In our society the open, innocent person ends up being badly hurt. But we often push this suppression of natural openness too far. Perhaps because of our own anxieties related to pleasure, we often suppress our children's capacity for joy even within the safe contexts of our own families and circles of friends.

All this is crucial in understanding how the pleasurable emotion of joy can cause distress. Emotional first aid cannot forcibly extract joy from people. This would be emotional rape, a taking of what is naturally a gift. The EFA of joy is somewhat different from that of the other emotions. It consists mainly not of something we do to help the other person, but of something we do in ourselves. We open ourselves, let our own joy come to the surface. This opens the way for others.

Chronic distress in the blocking of joy lies so deep that the way open is more difficult. Some people have become so depressed that their daily lives are dominated by melancholy, inertia, and envy. Their bodies are in such a state of deflation and subservience to gravity (need to lie down frequently, difficulty in maintaining erect posture) that they can only watch the opening of other people to joy as if from a great distance. Even a temporary blocking of joy because of embarassment or fear of envy often has the outer signs of depression: lowered voice, slumped posture, fallen facial features. This is the opposite of the antigravity elation of joy.

Provocation (Envy)

This must be discussed from a different angle than with the other emotions, since provocation of others to joy is hardly a problem. Instead, joy becomes blocked because of fear of disapproval or malice from others. The various provocations of the blocking of joy can be summed up under the heading of envy.

Envy, at its roots, is a longing for joy observed in others. (The word 'envy' originates in a Latin word for desire.) A sociologist, Helmut Schoeck, has made a classic study of how the ramifications of envy are felt in all societies, causing elaborate rituals of envy avoidance. Most of us must know the instinctive feeling that if we show our joy too much we are inviting some kind of reprisal or revenge from others. It is almost a superstitious feeling, of the 'evil eye' that might see our pleasure and resent it. We have a word, 'killjoy,' for people who overtly suppress the joy of others. Envy is often more subtle, and at the same time easy to forget because of its omnipresence. But we placate it instinctively, downplaying our pleasure at success or at new discoveries or acquisitions. And we join the side of envy each time we dismiss as boasting a person's innocent expression of pleasure in achievement.

Why is envy so omnipresent? Schoeck places its roots in sibling rivalry, but not all siblings are envious. I would propose that envy is in direct proportion to a person's sense of deprivation. A person who has grown up in what Reich called an 'emotional desert' of lack of love and warmth experiences nothing but inner pain at the sight of another's pleasure, as this awakens the stirrings of longing ('envie' in French), which press for release but are blocked. A vicious circle occurs, since envy from others makes it even less likely that newly awakened joy will be allowed to emerge.

Depression is such a common disease in our society, rightly evoking sympathy and care, that its deep content of envy often goes ignored in the interest of this care. It is somehow more acceptable to draw on the psychoanalytic evidence that depression contains a large element of blocked anger than to acknowledge the even larger element of blocked desire for contact. It is even harder to acknowledge that blocked desire turns readily into killjoy behavior, which is based in envy.

Because of its associations with morality and the commandments, envy is something of a taboo subject. But if its roots in deprivation and blocked desire are realized, it can perhaps be seen as an unfortunate condition rather than simply as a vice, and some effort can be made to release it from its place in the person's character structure. This can be done in therapy by awakening in the person the very capacity for pleasure and joy that his or her envy normally seeks to destroy in others. In EFA, it is important to recognize envy in order, at least, to identify it in the person and try to explore its roots in blocked longing.

Contact (1)

The element of contact, so essential in the EFA of blocked grief, fear, or anger, becomes in the EFA of blocked joy a more active kind of sharing. In fact, the EFA of blocked joy can best be summed up in the word 'share.' This operates on several levels:

—If a person is outwardly depressed while communicating a

joyous message, *share your joy* in their joy. This will give permission and, by infection as it were, possibly open their own expression of joy.

—If a person is outwardly depressed while observing someone else's joy, the same rule applies. If you share your joy, you may help open up theirs.

Words may touch and release any component of envy present in the other person if you confront it directly with a remark acknowledging your own *desire* mixed with pleasure at what a third party has. For example, 'I must say, I'd really like to have a house like that myself.'

The onset of joy is so quick that the normal EFA of making a preliminary contract cannot apply. It would be ridiculous to say 'Can I help you express your joy?' All you can do is make a verbal or physical gesture of sharing the joyful situation. If this does not work, there is nothing further to do.

In cases of depression that seems unjustified in the face of a basically positive situation, the basic verbal approach, touching possible feelings of envy and deprivation, is to ask 'What do you want?' 'Isn't there anything you'd like to have or do right now?' You might contract, in a cheerful or joking sort of way, to help try to cheer the person up, but this involves physical movement (see following section). A key question in identifying whether signs of depression are covering up suppressed joy, or at least the desire for pleasure, is whether there is a discrepancy in the person's expression and the content of what he or she is saying. If the content is relatively positive or cheerful, in spite of a gloomy expression, it may be worth pursuing the direction of joy. More often the content will be as gloomy as the expression, and the EFA of grief or anger may be called for.

Contact (2)

You can, of course, share joy through touching or embracing the person, if your relationship permits. Apart from this, in cases of depression, it may be worth trying to stimulate the person to a movement of expansion or reaching out, to 'lift' the person, attempt to raise their spirits. You might, in a light manner, try to get the person moving as follows:

—Ask them to stand up and spring up and down slightly with the weight on the balls of their feet.

—At the same time, encourage them to look around actively as if searching.

—Ask them to pull their shoulders back and to inflate their chest fully as if breathing in fresh air. Not to hold the breath, simply to take it in fully and hold it for a moment as if relishing it, then letting it out with an open sigh.

—It may help to encourage the person to open the hands and reach outward as if to embrace the world.

—Encourage a wide open smile.

Make sure the eyes participate in the smile. Have the person make some faces to loosen the muscles of the cheeks and then let the eyes narrow and the corners turn up along with the smile.

All this is an act, up to a point, but as with other simulations, it may open the organism to the channeling of the emotion. Done with good humor, making faces and artificial gestures may awaken some latent pleasure from whatever parts of the person have become temporarily dead with depression.

You may even have the person jump up and down. A final maneuver, which may seem ridiculous at first but is often stimulating, is to hold hands facing each other and jump up and down letting out short 'Ah!' sounds. Children spontaneously do this in such games as Ring-around-the-roses.

Switching

Sometimes a person is overwhelmed by joy, and the soft expansion of emotion causes a rush of tears to the eyes. This is distinguished from grief by the fact that the eyes remain open to take in the source of the joy and share it. Joyful people look at each other through their tears.

However, the tears may turn to genuine sobbing and hiding

of the eyes, in a switch to grief. This is natural. Many occasions of joy contain an element of grief because of previous loss. After all, when you are overjoyed at meeting a long departed friend, the surge of contact and emotion may recall the original loss that was experienced with grief. Particularly, if this former grief was not fully expressed at the time, it may emerge now.

Resolution, problems, emergency

The main problem in resolution after an expression of joy is embarrassment at having been too open or intimate. All you can do here is to continue to express your own openness and permission, and share your own joy with the person.

Other problems have already been mentioned. Emergency may seem impossible with joy, but cases are on record of people having fainted or died from an intensity of joy. One theory has it that a surge of joy in a person who habitually suppresses it with a rigid armor of control is too much for the organism, and particularly the heart, to take. Such cases are apparently rare. And it would seem that a genuinely soft movement of joy could do no harm to a person who accepts it. Frantic, frenzied jumping around is a flight from this soft expansion, and basically must be treated as fear. As always, contact and breathing low in the abdomen will calm the person. Permission and sharing may then open the road to the joy that has been blocked, so often by fear.

8

Children/Parent Crises

EFA with children

The dynamics of emotional expression in children and in adults
are the same. In fact, by observing the emotions of children, we
can learn a lot about the truth underlying many adult emotional
expressions that are covered over by a superstructure of many
layers of defense. Much Emotional First Aid with adults consists of trying to reach through the superstructure to basic emotions that come out simply, by comparison, in children or even
in animals. Emotions in children are usually instantly recognizable. Emotional distress, in the sense of the conflicts, tensions,
muscular rigidities and restraints that keep a particular emotion
particularly blocked in an adult, is not even observable in very
young infants. For them, distress is not blocked emotion, it
is itself an emotion—an amalgam of grief, fear, and rage at being
deprived of contact. In young infants, emotions can be more
accurately described as needs. Once the need is identified, and it
is usually a simple one, the only possible measure is to satisfy
it. This may be true of adults also, but the superstructure hides
the underlying need, which EFA must work to find and satisfy.

Older children (after the age of, say, four) who have experienced separation from the mother, loss, and autonomy, are
more like adults. They show the same emotions, only more intensely. Few adults retain the mobility and sensitivity of children. EFA with children is essentially similar to that with

adults, and the same measures to aid discharge of accumulated tension can be used. But the guidelines for use are different, because of the greater fragility and sensitivity of children. It is rather like adjusting a dose of a drug: a 'dose' of active EFA intervention, which would not harm an adult, might emotionally overpower a child. Every intervention, whether verbal or through movement and touch, has to be lighter.

It is up to parents' own judgment how to integrate the EFA methods described earlier with the reality of who their child is, and with their expectations for the child. The aim of this chapter is to offer some guidelines for EFA with children based on an understanding of their emotional development. It would be impossible to sum up this development in a single chapter, but the following sections will at least give an overview. (See *Suggested Further Reading*). The final sections of the chapter will note some specific problems that occur between couples, and draw attention to the possibility of EFA during childbirth.

The emotions of the newborn

A one-day-old baby awakes from a period of sleep in its cradle or in bed beside the mother. Its legs and arms begin to undulate as it utters soft cries. Its eyes move back and forth searchingly. The undulating movements of the limbs, and the cries, become more vigorous. Several things can happen now, depending on the mother's response:

—The mother goes to her child, picks it up, makes loving sounds, and puts the baby to the breast. The baby roots for the nipple, sucks firmly for a while. The limbs undulate slowly. The baby makes soft sounds. Its body seems to glow, the skin pink. Its eyes may look up at the mother. After a while its face, head, and body tremble with satisfaction, and it drifts off to sleep again, snuggled in toward the mother's skin. By a few weeks later, after the same experience, its face will show a serenely joyful smile.

—The mother ignores the baby. Nobody comes. The cries become louder, the movements of the limbs become harsher. The skin becomes red, the baby seems puffed up. Its eyes may look around wildly but more likely are squeezed shut with the crying that takes on a grating sound. The limbs push out, and the back arches. After a while it stops from sheer exhaustion and drifts off into a kind of sleep. The face seems wizened and contracted, the skin bluish.

—The mother picks up the baby and forces a bottle of cold formula into the baby's mouth. The baby's back arches and it regurgitates the fluid instantly, the lips pushing outward. It utters a strangled cry.

—The mother picks up the baby roughly. The arms and legs shoot out abruptly, the eyes stare open blankly. The quick but gentle breathing is disturbed for an instant. The body area seems to shrink, all the breath briefly gathered into the chest. The skin is pale.

This is approximately the emotional range of a day-old newborn. In the first example, the baby's emotion can be described as joy, in the special sense that it begins with a softly expressed need for contact and ends up with a full, soft expansion of the organism and a trembling discharge in satisfaction. In the second example, the baby's emotions can be broadly called anger, although it is more of a generalized distress that contains elements of anger, fear, and what will later (when the baby realizes what loss is) become grief. In the third example, the emotion can also be called anger, in the special sense of disgust and rejection. In the fourth example, the baby's reaction is fear, including the startle reflex and the instinctive fear of falling that babies show when handled roughly. Even if they are too young to know what falling actually is, their reaction resembles that of young primates whose bodies contract into a ball as they fall from trees.

These emotions have been described, in more developed form, throughout this book. But it should be clear that here there is no question of EFA. All that is required is that the mother satisfy the infant's need, by gathering the infant to her body and allowing the natural reflex of rooting for the breast to take its course. Later, other needs, such as to be changed or rocked, may be expressed. But always each need contains the message of how it can be satisfied. Nothing is complicated.

But even this simple expression of needs is sometimes not recognized as *emotional*. Instead, when the baby cries, it is assumed that 'it needs to be fed.' Some babies are conditioned early to learn that they will only find response when they are hungry, and that the response will last no longer than it takes for them to be fed. They may eventually quiet down after a period of protest and distress: they are depressed babies. Or the distress continues: they are angry babies. They are handled roughly when they protest: they become frightened babies.

Even the most progressively caring treatment of babies often turns out to be conditional because of emotional expectations or blocks in the parents. An example is a well known 'hippie' community known as 'The Farm.' All the births are 'natural,' (unmedicated), and the mothers breastfeed their babies on demand until the baby weans itself in its own time. This sounds excellent. But evidently, the mothers' response to the babies' demand is systematically conditional. Since the philosophy of the Farm is 'nonviolent' (meaning anger is not permitted), the babies are never put to the breast until *after* they have stopped crying. To satisfy their cry would be to encourage angry demanding. The babies soon learn to cry less, since they are only satisfied when they are quiet. The mothers probably do not know that there is a risk of this being counterproductive. One study of a tribe of Alaskan Eskimos, who used to follow exactly the same 'taming' principle with their children, links this practice of conditional breastfeeding with a constant tendency in adult Eskimos of this tribe toward violence, the suggested explanation being that the adults retain the suppressed rage they have felt as children.

In other words, people's acceptance or rejection of the basic emotions not only affects the quality of their contact with each other, it affects the kind of character structure their children develop.

Mothering and parenting

Mother gets the blame for everything. This may seem unfair. So much therapy or psychoanalysis teaches people to express their long buried hatred of their mothers that this has become a kind of tragic joke. In defense even of harmful mothers, it must be admitted that women with children do not have an easy time. Only forty years ago they were bullied by their male doctors into thinking that it would damage the child's character if they picked it up except for feeding at predetermined intervals. It is not easy to buck authority, especially since child rearing is invested with so much responsibility and anxiety. The modern tendency is for everything, from birth to bottle to daycare center, to be completely mechanized. In some primitive societies, which we mistakenly see as idyllic, nothing much is mechanized, but mothers are prevented by envy and ritual from handling their infants with any special tenderness. In many societies, the very real emotions of the infant are not recognized. The fact that they are needs means that they can be misinterpreted as merely mechanical needs for the right temperature, the right food, the right amount of sleep. All this is surely an extension of the downplaying of emotions among adults, except for certain ritual occasions, and since the mother is the main transmitter of society's values in the early months of childhood, it is she who later gets the blame for the whole problem.

The fact remains that there are specific needs of young infants (up to the age of about three), and especially the need to be nursed at the breast, which can only be satisfied through the mother, or failing a mother, a mother substitute. This means that the mother—meaning the mother's own organism, the skin of her body, the way she moves, the sounds of her voice, her emotional responsiveness—becomes the initial reference point for all subsequent emotions. She is ground zero, as it were, the place where all emotions are first experienced and take off from. Many studies have shown that a baby deprived of its mother in the early months is actually deprived of its emotions. After initial phases of protest and despair, all that remains is detachment.

Again, there is no question of Emotional First Aid as such. But the mother's satisfaction of the child's needs can be seen as a kind of prototype. With adults, EFA provides the kind of support that a child needs from its mother. A mother's acceptance of the infant's needs means acceptance of the infant's emotions.

But mothers are surrounded by social pressures to reject the infant's needs. The conventional wisdom is that responses should be conditional, not unconditional, or that the child should have token access to the breast (i.e. at certain times only) rather than unrestricted access. It is as if there is a fear that given complete freedom, the child will completely devour and consume the mother. Indeed, if the mother is not strongly supported by her mate and the rest of her family, she may feel this way. Not all are strong enough, or have support enough, to be completely accessible.

When the mother is completely accessible, it turns out that she is not devoured after all. The child becomes fully satisfied, emotionally as well as physically, and a pulsation of contact and withdrawal imposes itself. (This is similar to EFA with adults; no matter what intense emotions are being expressed, though it seems they will continue for ever, they will always be resolved if there is an adequate response.) This process was called by Reich 'self regulation,' and was the basis of the child education methods of A. S. Neill at Summerhill. As Neill continually had to point out, self regulation means 'freedom but not license.' An organism that is self regulating does not in fact make excessive demands on others, although at times it may certainly make strong demands that cry to be met.

At the primary level, of needs demanding satisfaction and diminishing after being satisfied, in a pulsation of contact/withdrawal and attachment/detachment, all emotional self regulatin begins with the contact with the mother. If she can be present and alive in her own organism, her child will develop a capacity for contact and an emotional liveliness.

By the time the father figures prominently in the child's emotional life, the child is more independent, and emotional expression has become somewhat different from the simple expression of needs. The child now experiences loss and frustration consciously in the sense that the child is aware of being able to satisfy its own needs at times, and is therefore more aware of the implications of being satisfied or denied by others. Relationships become more complex. Parenting, whether by mother or father, becomes a constant balancing act between self regulation of the child and parental regulation in the interests of health and protection. Some sort of EFA, or at least emotional awareness, becomes useful.

Self regulation and emotions

There is no space here to take into consideration all approaches to parenting. It will be assumed that most readers of this book have some respect for self regulation in children, since an interest in Emotional First Aid would seem unlikely in a person who was dedicated to methods of disciplining or indoctrinating children.

EFA as so far explored is consistent with self regulation in that it encourages the organism to seek its own emotional direction, and tries to remove some of the blocks, rather than suggesting directions for the organism to take. But we all want to protect our children, and there is a strong temptation to keep them safe from harm by directing them. This section will note some commonly expressed problems in this area.

Sibling rivalry. Whether to interfere in battles between children concerns many parents, and has been one of the most common questions at classes on EFA. Since sibling rivalry is an element in the development of the killjoy condition of envy, this may offer a clue as to how to resolve it. It seems to depend usually on feelings of deprivation by one of the children concerned. The first EFA measure must be to identify how the child is unhappy, what the child *wants*—especially from the parents. This may seem a tangential approach, but may resolve the underlying issue.

In the heat of battle between siblings, emotions run so high that it is tempting to put a stop to the conflict completely. This kind of interference (although obviously legitimate in the case of impending injury) tends to lead to a build up of resentment, and later explosions when the parent is out of the way. The other extreme, of encouraging some kind of controlled showdown between the warring children, is not advisable. One child is usually stronger than the other and will always win. This is distressful enough for the younger or weaker child without being reinforced by a staged confrontation that the adult watches. This is an example of how guidelines for EFA with children must be different from those with adults. For a child, the adult is a figure of huge power. A major 'Don't' for adults in the EFA of children must be: *Don't manipulate children.*

Although sibling rivalry is a classic situation where the adult is tempted to use power to resolve the issue, it might be best to realize that for all children their parents are a more important emotional reference point than their brothers or sisters. The needs expressed in the sibling rivalry are in the last analysis needs for some sort of contact or attention from the father or mother. Sibling rivalry can therefore best be resolved in a child's talks with the parents when the other child is absent, not about the rivalry, but about the child's needs.

Frustration. Life is full of frustrations for children, and parents are the instruments of the frustrations. This is sometimes reasonable, in the interest of protection, and sometimes unreasonable. It is not wrong to say no to a child. But if the child reacts angrily, it is wrong to condemn the reaction. In other words: *Don't frustrate frustration.*

Respect and condescension. It is hoped that the examples of childhood and adult emotional behavior presented in this book will demonstrate that at the level of the basic emotions there is no difference between adults and children. Most of us know this theoretically. But we forget it because we are bigger. A child's rage does not seem so deep as ours because it is often about something that, to us, seems trivial. But it is better for us to forget the content and open ourselves to the expression. When a child loses a toy, the expression of grief and anger may amount to a feeling as strong as our own feeling when we have lost a job. It is the emotion, not its content, that counts. And the child may be more overwhelmed by the emotion than an adult. All this is a question of respect. *Don't condescend to children.*

Further problems will be discussed under the headings of the basic emotions.

Grief

Grief as we know it in adults does not exist in infants under the age of about six months. They do not react to loss with a soft, sobbing contraction of the body. Instead, after an initial period of protest, they become immobile, dazed, with blank searching eyes. The same expression can be seen in mother-deprived monkeys. At these early ages, loss of mother equals loss of the emotions, and the infant will grow up emotionally empty.

Grief as such begins to be seen when a child is aware of loss. If it is the loss of mother, for a child in the first years of life, the cycle that John Bowlby *(Attachment and Loss)* has identified as protest—despair—detachment, will occur. The specific grief reaction is seen in relation to loss that is emotionally overwhelming but not annihilating. An example would be the breaking of a favorite toy, or the death of a much loved pet. A child crying after this kind of loss seems to experience it with infinite poignancy, as if the whole world has been taken away. But the child does recover emotionally, and what is very important, he or she retains the capacity to feel grief and express it. The loss has not erased the emotion itself. I would propose that the reason for this capacity to integrate the experience of loss is that the child still has its mother. Mother is not lost. The child still has a secure reference point and source of support and contact. There is an important lesson here for adult EFA: a person will retain the capacity to discharge tension through the emotion of grief, provided he or she feels basically secure. For an adult, a secure sense of the self has replaced the need for mother. This security may be shaken by grief, and EFA can provide a temporary support. But the EFA works because the person has an inner security to return to. It is notable that people who have little or no sense of security, or who feel emotionally deprived, very often cannot cry. It would be too dangerous.

When a child cries from loss, the instinctive reaction of a warm-hearted parent is to gather the child into his or her arms. Often the child is lifted to the adult's shoulder, and the adult lays one hand on the back of the neck and comforts the child with a rocking motion—instinctive EFA. It is a mistake for an adult to try to cheer up a child. The child will sense if this is in fact to relieve the adult's own anxiety. A child's emotional expression can be frustrated directly by commands or threats to stop, or indirectly by the nonverbal message that the emotion makes the parent uncomfortable. All the emotional distress that EFA with adults aims to help has its origin not in childhood emotions as such—children are resilient enough to survive many emotional traumas—but in the frustration of the emotional expression itself.

The classic threat that crushes grief in a child is: 'Stop crying or I'll give you something to cry about.' What child, or even adult, could survive this double message? But it is heard frequently. It also reappears years later when the adult is in therapy trying to find out what has caused feelings of deadness. As one person in therapy, incapable of crying, said to me: 'When I was a kid I would be spanked, then I would cry, then I would be spanked again for crying.' In such cases, the block is visible in the clenched jaw, tight neck and shoulders, and the hard chest over a hardened heart.

Anger

The frustration of frustration. This is the key to the blocking of anger in children. A child's anger is intense, even frightening, to those who pay attention to it. It is just as powerful as the anger of an adult—understandably, since both are emotions that fill the whole organism. As usual there is no essential difference between the emotions of child and adult. But when an adult becomes fully angry, onlookers are likely to retreat. When a child becomes angry, the same onlookers may laugh or brutally scold the child. A whole social superstructure of authority and obedience reinforces this. A cynic might say that this is because the violence of a child is less threatening than that of an adult. The child can be crushed without danger. But in fact, adult violence is not simply an extension of anger, it is a result of blocked anger. The origins of this block can be seen in examples from childhood. Typically, a boy will be brutally beaten back when he tries to express anger toward a parent. In frustration he rushes to hit another child, or to find a dangerous weapon, or to destroy some precious object. In later life he may turn up in therapy as the sort of dangerous bar fighter who goes blind with rage when insulted by someone he perceives as stronger, and rushes for the nearest broken bottle or knife. Sober, he is afraid of his own anger. He has both been punished for it, as a child, and seen the results of his own violence, which he mistakenly identifies as anger. Violence is impotent, but anger can be potent if allowed its voice. Children and their emotions are seldom allowed to show any potency. After all, if a child's anger were taken seriously, adults might be influenced by it to modify their behavior, and for the average, insecure adult this would be humiliating.

So it still occurs that boys in particular grow up with the heavy muscle-bound shoulders that contain anger, and the furtive eyes that are afraid to look directly in case their inner wish for violent revenge can be seen. In girls and women, the suppressed anger tends to emerge in the form of arrogance, cutting remarks, and masochistic maneuvers. This is not biological. Men and women, adults and children, are equally capable of anger. But once a primary emotion is suppressed, the various secondary reactions that remain (in the case of anger these are resentment, guilt, hatred, remorse, etc.) are channeled by cultural expectations. The men are expected to be potentially violent, the women potentially malicious.

Though a child's anger is disturbing in its intensity, the best gift you can offer is acceptance. Of course, when the chips are down, the child is impotent compared to the adult, but leaving brute force aside, an adult who feels genuinely big inside should be capable of giving in to a child's anger if it makes sense, and of at least respecting it when it does not.

The methods of EFA for anger with adults can be used cautiously with children, with the exception of those that imply showdowns. In particular, it may be useful to help the child be aware of the legitimacy of his or her anger by encouraging the child to look directly at the adult. 'Let me see how angry you are' is a fair request to a child. And to make the emotional conflict more equal, it helps if the adult crouches or sits down at the child's level so that they are eye to eye.

Some parents encourage their children to take out their anger on a specific toy or doll as a scapegoat, in the interest of avoiding general destruction. This is well meaning, and accepting of the child's anger, but it is also controlling and does nothing to relieve the child's sense of impotence. The child knows perfectly well that kicking the doll is an artificial substitute. And kicking or beating a doll is an unfortunate prototype for adult violence. I would suggest a two-step approach to destructive anger in a child:

—First, encourage a direct statement from the child to the person who is responsible for the child's resentment (let us say the parent who has forbidden a treat). Encourage, but don't bully, the child to look the parent eye to eye on the same level, to show the anger.

—Second, propose some kind of vigorous activity to mobilize whatever anger remains. 'Let's go and kick a ball around, and let off steam' is a fair idea. Sharing the activity with the child respects the emotion. And a ball is more appropriate for kicking than a scapegoat doll.

Many parents may say such a proposal is naive. The realities of interaction with a three-year-old are more complex than anything this book can express in a few examples. True, but simple principles are still valid, such as 'Don't intimidate, don't manipulate, don't bully.' And they all reduce to one basic principle: respect the child's emotions as much as you would your own.

Children are certainly maddening. Part of the problem of children's anger is the anger it arouses in adults. Is it right to show your anger fully to a child? The fact that many adults recall their parent's rage with vivid terror indicates a need for caution. An adult's blazingly angry eyes can threaten to destroy a child.

If you respect a child's emotions, you have the right to demand that the child respects your own emotions. It is honest to express your anger. But a rule to follow might be to respect the proportions of the situation and not to show your anger to a child more intensely than you think the child is capable of showing its anger to you. Of course, show anger with your eyes, but don't kill with your eyes. Enough children have been emotionally killed in this way already.

Finally, the old question: is it right to hit a child? This is relevant to EFA and to anger, because your expressions of anger toward the child determine the range of the child's own future expressions. The simple answer to this question is: 'No.' Hitting converts anger into violence. But many of us who have children would say it is not quite so simple. We may have hit our children, especially when the child has given us a fright through some dangerous action. And it can be emphasized that to strike a child in anger is not the same as to beat a child deliberately as part of a technique of punishment. Corporal punishment is always violence, whether private or institutionalized.

I would propose that it is basically wrong to strike a child in anger because it is violent and because there is a danger that the adult's superior size is being used to intimidate the child. Intimidation is the foundation for later fear, impotence in anger, and chronic violence. But on occasion, it does seem fair to strike our children. The example that comes to mind is retaliation when our children strike us. If your daughter kicks you on the shin and it hurts, is it really wrong to hit her back? If she has given you a fright by running in front of a bus, is it really wrong to smack her once to reinforce your angry statement of concern? These questions must be for parents to decide, perhaps after discussions with the children themselves. It is possible, though, to establish a simple guideline for the physical expression of anger to a child: never strike a child with any more force than the child would be capable of exerting. That is, if you hit an eight-year-old child, be sure that you are hitting no harder than an eight-year-old would. The result may not be a blow but a forceful tap. It will, however, express your anger. It will also show the child that anger can be expressed in a focused and controlled way. You mitigate your anger in choosing to express it on the child's own level. The tap is not violence, but a forceful expression of anger.

My own view is that, if adults respected the anger of children and responded honestly while taking care to keep their response at the children's own level, this would be a step toward the rehabilitation of anger as a legitimate and nonviolent human emotion. But I have to state this personally rather than as an authority or a therapist. The whole question is delicate.

Fear

Fear of falling and fear of separation from mother seem to be the earliest fears, and they are associated since all falling is away from mother. Other early fears, such as of looming figures, of being alone in the dark, or of abrupt movement, can also be linked with the basic fear of falling. This may be why, even for an adult, the cures for fear are support, reassurance, and comfort—exactly what a child receives from its mother.

The response to fear in a child is as self evident as the response to grief: to offer contact, warmth, and acceptance. But adult fear of fear often blocks this. How many adults who harshly refuse a nightlight to their frightened children would be honestly unafraid of being left alone at night in a dark field? To a small child, a room is as unknown and almost as big as a field.

The world of an adult is very sure. Childhood fears seem irrational and ignorant by comparison. I can remember as a small child, by myself, seeing an enormous fireball descend during a thunderstorm and burst with a pop above the pavement. When I told my parents, they answered that 'according to scientists, fireballs do not exist,' but now that I had seen one, they knew that fireballs *did* exist. I am grateful. It took science another twenty years to admit that fireballs, although theoretically impossible, do exist. This is to me an example of trust: my parents trusted me in this instance, even though I was frightened. I could therefore trust them. Trust, for a child, is linked to resolution of fear. Mistrustful, paranoid adults have usually been deeply frightened as children and have received no reassurance. Even worse, sometimes the parents to whom they turn for reassurance are in themselves dangerous and frightening. The worst 'double bind' of all must be for a child to run frightened to a parent and then be received with frightening anger.

The adult's fear of the child's fear is as destructive as the frustration of frustration. In some children, the development of specific emotions simply comes to a halt. As always, the parent's acceptance of an emotion in his or her self is the only guarantee that it will be accepted in the child. This is why it is so important for adults to share their emotions with their children, even if the emotion is fear. Even children two years old can be seen consoling a parent who shows grief or fear. Of course, it would be wrong for the parent to place him or herself repeatedly in a position of needing to be mothered by the child. The child needs the parent to be strong, but also human. We often become inhuman because of our fear of our own emotions. As one patient in therapy said wonderingly, 'How could I be so frightened of just me?'.

There is no need to propose simulations of fear for a child, since the experience of fear is rarely blocked. (If it *is* blocked, and the child is often frozen or paralyzed with anxiety, it would be overwhelming to attempt to activate the underlying fear.) Chronic fear or anxiety in a child require professional help, since they usually overlie some family situation which the parents cannot be objective enough to resolve with the child.

For acute fear or anxiety in a child, the best initial advice to an adult must be: 'Think small.' *Be* the child, identify with it. The fear will be easy to understand. Then become an adult again, and offer support from your strength.

Joy

At first glance, it is difficult to imagine how joy can be repressed in children—they are so full of it. Babies actually shriek with joy, as their hands shoot out and their faces light up. Perhaps an uninhibited adult would also shriek. But this is usually suppressed in the first years of life. A shriek from a two-year-old becomes more noisy than that of a baby. It compels attention. The two-year-old may also jump up and down, or roll on the ground and jump up again. How many parents allow this? A cynic might say that the joy of babies is tolerated because the volume of their shrieks is limited and, besides, a happy baby is

flattering to its parents since they must be the source of the joy.
A two-year-old, however, may be joyful about something else
altogether—the appearance of a cat walking across the lawn or
the sight of another child throwing a ball. This joy, innocent as
it is, is often censored as if it were somehow indecent. It all
touches too much adult envy, envy-avoidance (what would the
neighbors think?) and pleasure-anxiety. Or the noise of a joyful
child touches the nerves of an adult who is depressed, that is,
lacking joy, and the layer of anger above the adult's depression
is activated.

Joyful children also tend to be dirty. They tend to take their
clothes off or to wear the same piece of clothing many days in
succession. They are saying yes to life, and this enables them to
say no when they are offered food or an activity that they do
not like. They are like primitives, self-regulating and unpredict-
able. And sometimes when they meet an adult, they reach out
and meet a wall.

A depressed child is very sad, but out of the reach of Emotional First Aid, since to be depressed so early in life means that
things have gone seriously wrong. Children should not need to
be cheered up. They are naturally already cheerful. If they have
lost their primordial joy, the only thing to bring it back is not
EFA, but love.

There is only one way to share joy with a child, and that is—
be a child. Forget your sober self, forget what other people
might think, and become what you really are underneath. The
child will recognize this.

Couples

The sections in previous chapters that discuss Expression,
Distress, and Provocation may be useful for couples. Emotional
First Aid measures are only valid for third-party situations, not
as a means of unravelling the complexities of a relationship in
its ups and downs. It helps, however, to recognize emotional
expression and distress. And some of the material on Provocation can be applied to the dynamics of the traps in which some

couples become stuck because of reciprocity of character structure and blocks.

In the tango of a couple's relationship, one partner often leads. In some cases, the lead alternates according to the field of action. There are variations on the basic step. Some couples, in terms of character structure, are as different and complimentary as sun and moon. Others are more like those twin star systems where the stars rotate around each other but occasionally threaten to collide, with spectacular effects in the way of flares and radiation. Although, at any given time, society tends to impose a norm, the happiness of the couple basically depends on who they are, and the barometer of the happiness is what kind of sexual relationship the couple has. To return to the tango: who leads when and how is less important than whether the dancing couple move in a rhythm that is more energetic and rich than the sum of their two separate rhythms. Whether this is achieved through an identity of rhythm or through a complimentarity is immaterial. Both increase the charge.

The sexual relationship is effected by whatever emotional blocks exist in the relationship. There are physical reasons for this. Letting go to a shared orgasm with the partner means letting go of whatever muscle tensions in the body may be holding back emotion: orgasm is a pulsation that contains many smaller pulsations. If they are blocked, it is blocked. One major pulsation is that of contact and withdrawal. If a couple are out of contact emotionally, or stuck together in a relentless sticky concern that covers up anger, the excitement of coming together sexually after a period of separate activity is diminished. On the muscular level, if one partner has been wanting to cry but unable to express this, he or she may go to bed with a rigid chest and neck, and the abdomen may be held tight to restrain feelings of sadness. This blocks letting go to the excited breathing of sexual contact. This is true of any block: the horizontal barrier to the flow of emotion up and down the body is also a barrier to the flow of sexual sensation.

For this reason, many couples are aware of the connection between problems in their sexual relationship and the need to express blocked emotion. They tend to avoid sexual contact while they 'have something on their chest,' or they take measures to discharge the tension through expressing the emotion. Instinctively, they want to 'feel clear' before making sexual contact. Some of the measures discussed in earlier chapters may be of help here. EFA within the couple is most useful in its self-help dimension. It might be manipulation to assist your partner to express his or her anger. But you can use the same methods to help bring your own anger out.

Contact between the man and woman in a couple can be described on three levels:

Verbal

Emotional

Sexual.

Clearly the levels are interdependent. A character in a Tennessee Williams play remarks, pointing to the bed: 'When a marriage is on the rocks, there's the rocks.' This is an oversimplification given the fact that sexual surrender to the partner is impossible if there is no way open for emotional surrender, and in turn most couples reach at least an agreement to disagree in many areas involving words and ideas. A constantly recurring ideological argument, for example, is likely to hide a deeper emotional or sexual discontent. In a sense, the character in the play is right. The bed is the most honest place in the relationship, where the problems first show. It is difficult to keep up pretenses there for very long. It is also difficult to pretend at the emotional level. It is easier at the verbal level, which is why it is the most superficial level in terms of the real contact between the two organisms. Consequently, many people retreat to the verbal level: bad relationships can survive there, in earnest efforts to resolve cognitive dissonances and 'communications problems.'

This book has nothing to say about relationships at the cognitive level. But some knowledge of EFA, and thus of functioning at the emotional level, can help keep a relationship honest. Perhaps a further book can explore the possibility of Sexual First Aid.

Childbirth

Emotions are usually excluded from childbirth. This may seem like an extreme statement in view of the many photographs that exist of delighted fathers behind masks looking at their newborn infants. If the mother is not overmedicated or exhausted, she may also look delighted. More likely she is dazed. The baby very often just cries, its first emotions being fear and deprivation. There is a current tendency toward 'natural childbirth,' in which at least the mother is not too drugged to experience the event with joy, and after which the baby is encouraged to snuggle close to the mother rather than to be separated from her. As Leboyer's photographs show *(Childbirth without Violence),* this is much better for the baby, whose face looks serene and even joyful. But the first statement still holds true if childbirth is looked at as the whole event, starting with labor and ending with the birth, not just as the few minutes after birth itself.

Medicated childbirth might better be called 'technical birth,' since more than medication is involved: compulsory enemas, fetal heart monitors with electrodes screwed into the baby's scalp while it is still in the uterus and which immobilize the mother, delivery tables with stirrups, and dazzling lights. Even if, as is the modern fashion, the father is permitted to attend, there is very little for him to do, and the mother will be mostly out of contact in a Demerol haze. Many people conscious of emotional health try to arrange a mixed kind of birth, where the technical aids are not completely intrusive, and where some natural childbirth methods are used. Others go all the way with natural childbirth. But as it is taught in most prebirth classes, natural childbirth is *not* natural. It consists of educating the mother in a series of breathing techniques that will enable her to simulate medicated childbirth, only without the medications. In other words, usually the aim is the same—a pain-free, essentially emotion-free, controlled labor in which breathing and relaxation techniques take the place of anesthetics. Admittedly, being unmedicated is being free to feel emotions at all stages, and to enter into unimpeded contact with the baby. And some books on the natural methods do advise women that it helps to remain in emotional contact with the husband. Some, referring to methods from body-oriented therapies derived from Reich, even stress the need for keeping the mouth open and maintaining eye contact with the husband or helper during difficult phases, and encourage the woman to 'breath the baby out' rather than to push (although pushing may occur involuntarily). Some natural childbirth instructors are also sensitive to how an openness to the emotions leads to an open labor and delivery of the child.

In sum, it would be more accurate to say that in current practice there are three kinds of childbirth: technical childbirth; the kind of natural childbirth that aims to keep the mother *above* the experience of birth (it is sometimes known as 'psychoprophylactic' childbirth, meaning that the mind is used in the control of pain); and the kind of natural childbirth which aims to keep the mother *in* the experience. Emotional First Aid is useless in fully technical childbirth, useful as a standby in psychoprophylactic childbirth, and an organic part of natural birth. A fully natural childbirth, for modern Western women at least, is a deeply emotional experience. This may be because it involves the letting go of many emotional conventions. Advocates of psychoprophylactic childbirth often give examples of primitive women who give birth to children without pain and without any emotion. Whether this is desirable or not (and the lack of emotion suggests a measure of resignation in these women), it is hard to imagine in women of our society. In fact, the tendency of women to become overwhelmed by emotions during childbirth is traditionally well known, though feared. The image of women screaming in childbirth strikes terror into our hearts and has been used as justification for the advance of technical childbirth. The idea that perhaps it helps the woman to scream has apparently been lost. According to some sensitive obstetricians, much of the pain associated with childbirth can be traced more to emotional blockage and inhibition and the consequent physical tensions than to the essential pain of the process of opening up the birth canal. 'Tense woman, tense cervix' is a traditional axiom. Of course, medication can relax the cervix. But emotional contact and discharge can relax the woman.

A normal childbirth consists of three stages: a longish period of labor in which regular contractions open the cervix; a brief period known as 'transition' when contractions are irregular and the cervix opens the last few centimeters very rapidly; and a period of delivery when the baby is being expelled down through the vagina into the world. There is nothing predictable about the emotions during childbirth, but in broad outline:

—During labor, emotions may not be particularly intense, although sadness or anger may occur if the process becomes fatiguing. More likely in some cases, there is a general anxiety that produces some signs of 'freezing' and slows down the labor. Contact and support from husband or helper are essential during labor. This includes eye contact, which may not be necessary, or may even be annoying if the woman wants to curl up quietly and let the process unfold slowly, but which becomes necessary if the woman freezes. The best guideline is that if the woman expresses no emotion, it is not necessary to insist on eye contact. But if the woman does express emotion, whether anxiety, anger, or sadness, eye contact will help it discharge and let the organism *move*. This is consistant with EFA.

—During transition, pain may be intense and emotions powerful. Eye contact and breathing are as important as during any EFA emergency. It may be particularly useful to encourage the woman to express the fear or anger in the eyes, as in the simulations suggested earlier. It is also essential to encourage the woman to make sounds. It is not necessary to scream, although of course if she feels like screaming, she should be encouraged. But sounds open the throat and let the wave of breathing flow down the body. Some of the measures suggested in the EFA of grief, to keep mouth and jaw relaxed during crying, are useful to childbirth. In transition, most anxieties come to a head. Terror may be felt. Bad experiences from the past, with the woman's own mother, or even apparently from the woman's own birth or what she has heard of it, may come to the surface. During periods of panic, constant effort is necessary to have the woman remain in eye contact. Rage against the husband or the baby about to be born may emerge. Accept it all. Don't create it, any more than in normal EFA, but encourage it to surface once its presence is apparent.

—During delivery, the prevalent emotion is joy. It may at first be a harsh kind of joy, with a component of anger. The woman feels back in control of the process, and exerts a new-found power in pushing the baby out. Unfortunately, many midwives and nurses encourage a very harsh kind of pushing. This may lead to panic in some women—the new-found power is fragile—and if this occurs, eye contact is essential. Or the pushing may be angry, even hateful, with a kind of 'I'll show you' quality. Women who have had more than one child tend to experiment in later deliveries with pushing more gently. It is in fact possible to 'breath the baby out,' with pelvic movements similar to those of sexual intercourse, and many similar sensations. The spontaneous joy of delivery is often inhibited by false ideas of modesty and the rush of sensations normally associated with sex. Delivery can be, in fact, an orgastic experience. (This is emphasized by at least two woman writers, Kitzinger and Newton—see Suggested Further Reading.)

After a birth in which emotions have emerged into contact, and the woman may have opened some of her deepest feelings from her personal history for the first time to herself and her partner, and in which delivery is experienced as an ecstatic discharge of the excitement accumulated over months of pregnancy, there is no problem with sharing the joy. The baby, in being brought from the internal embrace of the uterus to the warm external embrace of its mother, is able to share in the joy too. It rarely cries, but reaches out softly, with its eyes, its voice making exploratory sounds, and with its whole body as it snuggles into the mother's skin.

The best use I can imagine for this book is for childbirth instructors and prospective parents, who can perhaps discuss the possibility of using EFA during childbirth, negotiating whatever contract seems best, while keeping in mind that the reality will always suprise them.

9

Questions about Emotional First Aid

Over the last four years I have given talks or day-long courses on EFA to various groups of people, through psychotherapy training programs, an institute for art therapy, and a university continuing education program. Most of these groups contain both professional helpers who want to apply EFA at work and people who want to apply it with family and friends. Some questions most often asked by professional helpers or counselors are discussed in the next chapter. This chapter addresses more general questions. But, of course, since counselors also are humans who have families and friends, and ordinary people are sometimes called upon for special help in emotional crises, the two categories overlap.

The questions discussed here have all been asked frequently at EFA courses. I have arranged them in the order in which their subject has been discussed so far in this book. There are no easy answers to questions about the emotions. My responses make no claim to be definitive. They are based on study and experience, but are naturally consistent with the theory of emotion and the framework for EFA which I have proposed. Most important is that the topics can be opened to discussion. The most rewarding EFA courses have been those attended by a relatively small number: a dozen or so people, with a balanced mix of men and women, who can raise exciting questions and begin to respond to them from their own experience. My own responses to the questions given here have been tested over the

years by being matched to the personal experience of several
hundred people who have engaged in vigorous discussions about
them.

Does grief ever stop?

This question is sometimes asked existentially: can we ever
be free of grief? Or sometimes more practically: is there some
average time period for grief to be worked through and done
with? Sometimes a person after a great loss, such as a death or
the breakup of a marriage, seems capable of crying forever.

Although life does not have to be a vale of tears, without
pain and grief it would be mechanical, or at least flat—"little in
joy, little in pain." It can be argued that without pain, no
species could have evolved, since the awareness of possible pain
is protective. For human beings, pain must include emotional
pain as well as physical. In the EFA of grief it helps to encourage the person to breathe *out* fully, right down to that agoniz-
ing place where sobs rack the body, and to urge the person:
"Let yourself feel the pain. It will be all right soon, but for now
let it hurt."

This is not sadism. Pain can be lived through. And if it is
denied, this is usually at a price. One woman said to me: "I have
not cried openly or shed a tear since I was a child. Instead I feel
the tears inside, trickling and burning down the back of my
throat." She had just been diagnosed as having a stomach ulcer
"of nervous origin." But even this conscious "crying inside,"
with an over-stimulated autonomic nervous system (one factor
in the genesis of stomach ulcers), is preferable to the autonomic
deadness of the person who has long suppressed even the sensation of grief, the "human machine" who is nevertheless prey to
deep, vague, disturbing longings. A poet, Charles Sorley, killed
in the First World War at the age of twenty, wrote:

> We have a dumb spirit within:
> The exceeding bitter agony
> But not the exceeding bitter cry.

Even a dumb spirit within is better than none. But EFA can help the "exceeding bitter agony" work itself through in a cry.

Overt grieving after a loss does stop eventually. Eventually hope and capacity for joy begin to emerge. After a few months, unless the person becomes stuck in a deep depression in which grief and anger are *not* being expressed, the worst is over. But who can say the grief from a severe loss should ever be finished? Almost all of us have experienced losses which even if in the distant past may still bring tears to our eyes when we think of them. This aliveness to past grief and openness to remembered pain do not have to stop us from experiencing pleasure now. Sometimes I meet people in therapy who have cut themselves off from past sadness in such a way that their memory contains huge gaps, or can be recounted simply as history—something that could have happened to someone else. But if we cut out chunks of our memory, or convert it to history, we are cutting out or denying parts of ourselves. Think of the poignant sadness of some of Mozart's music, or of Blake's Songs of Innocence and Experience. These are not merely howls of pain transposed into music or verse: the grief they express is mixed with elation and joy. The expression of grief does not block the capacity for joy, it opens the way. Of course, sustained joy is out of place when a loss has just occurred. But the EFA of grief has worked when the person has retained the *capacity* for joy—even if the loss will always be remembered with sadness.

Is anger really necessary?

Even when the consequences of blocked anger (see Chapter 5) have been understood, this question lingers, and is probably the most common asked in EFA courses. This seems to be because many people have been badly hurt by other people's anger, especially as children, and, in turn, hate themselves when their anger hurts others. The whole thing is ugly, and frightening, like the face of anger itself.

But I still maintain that anger is at its most ugly, violent, indiscriminate, and unjust, when it is mixed with fear. The face of anger is too often like the masks on the totem poles of Pacific Coast Indians: a distorted expression of loathing and horror, with the teeth bared in a snarl but the eyes open in terror. The totems scared off intruders not so much by expressing anger as because the manifest fear in the masks in turn evoked fear. In real, blazing anger, the face is flushed and extremely concentrated and determined, but not distorted as with fear. The genuinely angry person is *focused* and therefore *in control.*

One woman told me of her rage at her husband during a quarrel about a vital matter. He began to walk out of the room. She picked up a wine glass and threw it. It smashed against the wall near his head. "You could have killed me," he gasped. But as she quickly picked up the glass, she had said to herself: "This is a crystal goblet which cost $45. But it's worth it." And she aimed for the exact spot on the wall where it hit. There was no question of her missing and hitting her husband.

This was not a commendable act. The quarrel was out of hand. Perhaps the woman could have made her point earlier, and less dangerously. But it is an example of how a person capable of retaining a focus in anger can thereby retain control. Controlled focus through the eyes aids muscular control, as for example in archery or tennis. People are most dangerous when they panic. I was once standing with a lumberyard worker beside a pile of wood from which a non-poisonous snake suddenly slithered out. The man, apparently phobic about snakes, grabbed a slat of 2 x 4 lumber and, his face contorted by rage and terror, pounded the snake to death. He "beat it to a pulp," the end of the slat kicking up the dirt from wild and unaimed blows. One well-aimed blow would have been enough—if the snake had been dangerous in the first place. But for a minute or so this mild-mannered man had become a panic-stricken killer.

I would maintain that if a person is incapable of focused anger, he or she is also incapable of constructive aggression. (Town gossip, for example, referred to the lumberyard worker as "henpecked" by his wife.) Assertiveness training workshops miss this point, in not acknowledging that blocks to assertion are in turn based on blocks to anger. The capacity for anger does not mean a person is perpetually angry. On the contrary.

Often anger is used defensively to cover up fear. When the mask of anger is only skin deep, or partial, so that signs of fear are discernible, EFA can help—either to concentrate the anger into a genuinely effective expression of a need which has been denied; or in acknowledging the fear, which is often of rejection or weakness. But in extreme cases, the defensive anger has taken over completely: the person has a short fuse and blows up easily, will never admit to fear, sadness, or weakness, and sets out to eliminate all opposition. The person becomes so dominated by anger as to be paranoid. A humorous example of the very unhumorous process in paranoia occurs in *Winnie the Pooh,* when Tigger suddenly jumps at a tablecloth and wrestles it to the ground. Pooh asks: "Why did you do that?" Tigger replies: "It moved." Pooh says: "But it didn't move." Tigger replies: "It might have moved." Paranoia gives anger a bad name.

But the opposite to paranoia, a complete rejection of anger, can lead to severe physical consequences, as is acknowledged in psychosomatic medicine. One woman in an EFA class got into an argument with some other participants. At least, they were arguing—she was not. She was sitting very calmly in one of the upright wooden chairs in the circle, and very sweetly stating that she was never angry. She thought anger was bad, and she said she meditated, concentrating on positive imagery, in any circumstances which might provoke anger. This riled the other participants. One woman whose house had recently been vandalized, gave this as an example: "Wouldn't that make you angry?" "No," the first woman replied calmly. Then suddenly, with a bang, the chair she was sitting on broke into three separate pieces, throwing her to the floor. The other participants gasped, then involuntarily laughed. The woman scrambled to her feet as I helped her up: "I'm not angry!" she said, pushing my arm away, her eyes blazing. A down to earth explanation of this odd event would be that her muscular tension was such, as she denied ever being angry, that it put an impossible stress on the chair. But she was very lightly muscled. Whether her tension was physical or psychic, it was hardly healthy.

William Blake wrote:

> I was angry with my friend:
> I told my wrath, my wrath did end.
> I was angry with my foe:
> I told it not, my wrath did grow.

Is it useful to discharge anger by hitting a pillow?

Many people have done this "exercise" in therapy workshops or encounter groups, and been encouraged to continue it at home, "to get their anger out." For some it can become a regular way to "dump" anger. I have known two cases where the principle has been taken to the extreme. In each case a man built himself a special room at home, in which the walls, floors, and boarded-over windows were padded with thick mattressing. After work each day the man would go into the room, strip down to his shorts and go berserk—kicking and screaming and pounding the walls. But neither of these men would say boo to a goose. Both were mild and soft in everyday life, although deeply frustrated. The anger could not be mobilized toward other people. In one case, therapy and the abandonment of the padded room enabled the man to focus anger and direct it into assertion in daily life. The other man preferred the padded room to therapy.

These cases represent an absurd extension of the "safety valve" principle which many pillow-pounders have also adopted. But pillow-pounding is not adequate even as a safety valve. For one thing, it is seldom done with the eyes focused and with a frown. I have seen people pounding pillows with their eyes open in wild, unfocused panic—like the man pounding the snake. Eventually they became more frightened than ever—of their own anger. It would be best to focus the eyes on a point on the pillow, and frown while pounding. But there is still another drawback: the pillow is *soft*. To let out the hard emotion of rage onto a soft surface is again frightening, and ugly. It is like pounding a baby. It is much more appropriate to pound with a rolled-up newspaper on a hard surface. But even this, as I suggested in Chapter 5, is better as a way of exploring your capacity for anger, than as a regular exercise or safety valve.

Again the problem is at the level of the eyes. If you pound away with a rolled up newspaper on the back of a chair to express your anger to another person, you may find yourself superimposing their image on the surface you are pounding. But this eventually contributes to what we call in therapy an "eye-block": a cutting of contact during emotion. Focused anger demands a direction. It is probably best for the emotional health to direct anger to the person who has aroused it. But, of course, this is not always feasible. The consequences might be some kind of punishment, loss of a job, or unbearable pain to someone else. There is less harm in repressing the *action* of getting angry, than the *feeling*. If the feeling is acknowledged it may indeed press to be "taken out on something." Businessmen know this when, after difficult conferences, they go off and pound their rage out on a racketball- or squash-court. But they do not need to imagine someone's face on the squash ball. It is possible, quite consciously, to divert accumulated anger into vigorous activity.

"Consciously" is the key word. Some people can repress even the feeling of focused anger, which remains only as a kind of dull restlessness which demands discharge in compulsive ways. For example, daily jogging or swimming, both healthy activities in their own right, can become compulsive safety-valve discharges of emotional, or sometimes sexual pressure.

EFA's value in dealing with anger is that the therapy recognizes the anger expression even in those who deny it, and EFA recognizes the admixture of fear when this also is denied. Deeply buried anger is probably a matter for therapy. But when some mixture of anger and fear begins to break through habitual denial, and to cause the person distress, EFA can step in to focus the anger. Usually this helps the person realize that obstacles which have seemed insuperable can be effectively "attacked"—in the sense of assertion, or controlled aggression. EFA, as effective therapy, uses "anger explorations" not as regular exercises, but as a means of getting a person in contact with their anger before the emotion is effectively, and safely, directed elsewhere.

How can EFA deal with anxiety about examinations,
stage appearances, etc.?

This is another very common question which illustrates that for most people temporary anxiety and stage fright before important occasions are a greater problem than obvious panic or terror. My answer is to re-emphasize the connection which so often exists between anxiety and suppressed excitement. But even when understood, the problem does not easily go away. It may indeed be helpful to gag forcibly, to take a brisk walk, or to try and let off steam through some diversion. But even so, the gnawing anxiety in the stomach may remain. I do not think that any person who is autonomically lively can easily tolerate long periods of waiting. Extremely patient, phlegmatic people are often emotionally rather flat or dull. In the last analysis, stage fright is probably a function of character structure. It is a paradox that EFA is less effective in low-grade anxiety than in panic or terror. EFA works best when emotion is stirred up and ready to flow, so that the EfA can clear away the obstacles to the flow. But if the angry person represses or delays examining his or her feelings, the flow has nowhere to go. On the other hand, I do not believe that relaxing into diversionary activity does any harm. I have known people who have worked day and night before crucial university final examinations, and who have found themselves sitting in front of the paper, when the time came to write the examination, completely paralyzed and blank. Low-grade anxiety often leads to compulsive behavior which is counter-productive. I had a client in therapy who was a marathon runner. When he ran he would always breathe in a very harsh way, his jaw half-clenched, puffing and blowing so loudly that he noticed other runners tended to avoid staying alongside him. He was convinced, for various physiological reasons, that this was the most effective way to breathe. I thought it was a sign of anxiety, and challenged him to try running with his jaw slack, and breathing lower down into the abdomen. He was worried that this would slow him down. But when he tried it at the next marathon, he cut a few minutes off his time, and felt less tired afterwards.

The point is that very often mechanical procedures to reduce or deny fear—compulsive work-routines, incapacity to relax or take a break—themselves often reinforce low-grade anxiety. One way to reduce stage fright or examination fright may be to allow, not block, periods of panic which can flush out some of the fear. Another is to acknowledge the excitement being felt at the coming challenge.

Are there any emotional differences
between men and women?

Behind this question is usually the observation that "women cry more easily, men express anger more easily." Most people would agree with this, but they sense something wrong with it. Are these differences innate?

The short answer is that emotional differences between men and women are largely socially conditioned, not innate. It may be true that under some circumstances such as during the menstrual cycle and birth, women are more open to emotion than men (see the next section, on post partum depression), but this means emotion in general, not simply grief or anger. Men and women are physically similar in those parts of the body which most participate in emotion: the face which expresses it, and the throat and lungs and trunk from which breathing fuels and drives it. Although some medical textbooks still repeat that women are "chest breathers" and men "abdominal breathers," in so far as this may be true it is a social deformation: the anatomy of the male and female breathing systems is almost identical. It may be claimed that anger depends on a strong musculature, especially in back, chest and shoulders, and that men have this. But this is true of physical aggression, not of the anger expression which can come through with powerful intensity even in a small child. I have seen hundreds of men and women in therapy. Their rage, fear, joy and crying are in no way different.

Nevertheless, more men than women have difficulty in crying. And more women than men have difficulty in expressing anger. The causes are not hard to find. Most small boys are told it is not manly to cry; whereas most small girls are expected to cry easily. Most small boys can get away with angry behavior, even to the point of nastiness—"boys will be boys"; whereas most small girls when angry are seen as exhibiting unladylike and ill-mannered behavior. These attitudes survive into adulthood. Many men feel it would be soft to cry; so, of course, they cannot allow themselves to be soft in any circumstances—not in playing with children, making love, or responding to affection. But women are expected to cry frequently, even to "sob hysterically." Many men take out their tension in anger at those around them, and are forgiven as being "under stress." A woman doing the same thing will probably be labelled "bitchy."

These attitudes are those of a patriarchy. In current Western society they are breaking down somewhat, but the progress is socially fragmented. In the business environment which is becoming the model for all work, almost all emotion is suppressed, as both men and women are supposed to become corporate drones, although with the compensation of institutional narcissism—feeling important, glossily dressed, moving briskly in an internally climatized environment which gives them mysterious headaches and pains which have to be doped down for fear of explosion. In the home environment, and in the less formal workplaces, there is more emotional give and take, but this has no public status. Even children are not expected to be emotional in public. The current version of patriarchy ends up squashing public emotional expression in both men and women. But in private, and in the arena of the family, more men seem to be learning to cry, more women to rage openly.

There is still a common tendency, though, for the main *masking* emotion to be grief in women, anger in men. Typically, a woman who bursts into rage which then falters, will dissolve into tears. A man who feels impotent in the face of superior force or bullying will sometime later begin to bluster angrily. Since these reactions are socially expected, they often bring immediate advantage. The crying woman wins a condescending pity. The blustering man wins a temporary acquiescence. But neither is really satisfied! For the woman has really wanted to make her point. And the man has really wanted to be taken care of.

EFA is very helpful in these situations, since it enables the person to recognize part of the emotion which is being masked, and encourages the feeling's expression. First, though, on the principle of going with the surface emotion, if the masking emotion is encouraged to express itself fully, its shallowness will be revealed, and it will fizzle out so that the expression of the underlying and more powerful emotion may be grasped and grappled with.

Does EFA work with post partum depression?

Like any depression, a genuine post partum depression contains a mixture of suppressed emotions—mainly grief, longing, and rage. But sometimes these tend to break through. There is more a state of post partum *anguish,* in which the woman is swept by waves of longing, often for her own mother; sadness which is sometimes indefinable, sometimes linked to things which have gone wrong during pregnancy and birth; and rage, at the husband for being in some way inadequate, or even more irrationally, at the baby. No wonder these conflicting emotions are hard to endure. Some women have even become psychotic after birth, as a kind of flight from this unbearable vulnerability. Others become dully depressed, in the usual sense of the word. But most often the main characteristic of post partum anguish is the woman's complete lack of defenses against waves of emotion which might ordinarily be under control.

Although emotional distress is sometimes psychologically generated, there are known physiological causative factors, such as hormonal changes, which much not be ignored. It is tempting to look always for emotional causes for emotional distress. But sometimes emotional conditions, even if they are related to problems of daily life, are consequences of physical changes. An example is nausea and vomiting in early pregnancy. Some psychoanalytically oriented researchers claim to have isolated emotional causes, such as that the mother to be is emotionally rejecting the pregnancy, or recalling rejection from her own mother. But there is overwhelming evidence that the condition is physiologically based, and biologically functional in that it causes the woman to take extra care of what she eats and does. Similary, post partum anguish may be partly functional. The mother's exquisitely raw sensitivity and fussiness may help her take the best care of her baby's needs. When anger is directed at the baby itself, this is dysfunctional, but it may be a secondary result of frustration in the environment—the hypersensitivity of post partum anguish being thwarted and misdirected.

It is not usually realized, in a society where birth is dominated by technology and drugs, that birth is a radically "de-armoring" process, in which the mother's muscular defenses against feeling are dissolved or smashed through. An unmedicated mother (see Chapter 8) may be swept by many emotions during childbirth. Her body is in the grip of a process which seems larger than she. (I suppose the only way a man can understand this is to remember occasions where he has been racked by violent digestive cramps or vomiting: during such episodes the person can muster no resistance, and afterwards feels "weak as a kitten"). A woman after the huge experience of birth literally cannot muster her defenses. Muscular holding in the whole body, but most especially in the abdomen, pelvis, genitals and legs, no longer exists. The old muscular tensions reestablish themselves over the following months, as hormone replenishments return to normal. The hormones released during pregnancy have worked to soften muscles and reduce tonus, and this process is only reversed gradually afterwards. As the woman "armors up" again, defenses are largely re-established, and post partum anguish or depression disappears.

There is, I think, one lasting benefit from the de-armoring process of childbirth: in almost all women the abdominal and pelvic muscles do not completely regain their former state.

They may regain tonus, but much chronic rigidity has been permanently dissolved. Young girls with tight abdomens which suppress feeling, have after childbirth soft abdomens which are open to more feeling, including sexual sensation. And yet the aesthetic dictates of society require that they exercise frantically to get back their adolescent look—not only to "firm up their tummies," but to restore hardness and rigidity. Luckily, this does not usually work. I suspect the emotional depth and maturity of many women who have been mothers is partly due to the de-armoring process of birth. I have seen in therapy some mothers who have reacted to this process with an exaggerated girlishness, enforced by high and anxious breathing to keep above the feelings in the abdomen. But more often the mother's whole personality has deepened. This seems the more so, the less the birth has been medicated. When the mother can *live* the letting go of the armor, it is more complete because physical de-armoring has been accompanied by emotional release. The positive effects of the mother's letting go of armor physically may be vitiated by the heavily medicated mother's awakening into a sense of anxiety or panic.

There is evidence that post partum depression is more severe after heavily medicated births. The theory to explain this is that the birth has been somehow unreal and unlived, and the baby, therefore, seems more alien. My impression is that after a medicated birth there is more genuinely a depression, in which many feelings are suppressed, and which is long-lasting and *chronic*. After an unmedicated, natural birth, there is more the anguish I have described, in which a turmoil of emotions is expressed, and which is *acute*. Also, a mother who breastfeeds is less likely to direct her anger at the baby, but may do so at the rest of her family.

EFA can help greatly in post partum anguish, because as usual by gradually working down through layers of emotion as they present themselves, it moves the person out of the quagmire of mixed feelings and conflict. In post partum depression it may be more difficult to help the emotion flow, since it may be "frozen in." EFA during labor may diminish subsequent post partum anguish or depression. At least it is true, from discussions I have had with doctors and midwives who have assisted at natural births, that when emotions have been freely expressed during labor the mother is in better emotional shape after the birth. Emotional support during pregnancy, labor, and the months after birth is essential. Many mothers are labelled as having post partum depression because they seem to make "unreasonable" demands on those around them, and become upset when these are not met. But this may be a rebellion against the social milieu which may fuss about the birth to come, and the baby itself, but which gives little recognition to dedicated mothering.

Is it harmful to suppress a child's temper tantrums?

This is often a question involving the adult's survival. A parent can hardly resist trying to stop a temper tantrum if it occurs at a crucial time. This is, of course, often the case: the child stages a tantrum at precisely the time when it feels neglected in the parent's involvement with an urgent project such as preparing for an outing, making a meal, wrapping an important present for someone other than the child . . . I say "stages a tantrum" because of the quality of deliberate drama and trying for effect which often enters in. But this does not mean the feelings are faked. They are usually genuinely intense, but in a child the flow of feeling is so strong but fluid that it can often be directed to a specific effect, although it is impossible to stop. Many parents hate themselves for the harshness of their own voices or gestures in response to a tantrum, or to the whining period which so often precedes one, when the child's voice mounts higher and higher in pitch and seems to drill into the skull. Or the parents wonder if there is something wrong with a child who has tantrums. But this is unlikely. Any child, but especially an energetic one, will whine when frustrated or tired or hungry, and have outbursts of temper which become tantrums.

EFA measures are irrelevant to a tantrum. The emotions are in full flow. And it is a mistake to try and focus a child's anger prematurely, since a child's needs tend to be naturally huge and confused at times. The child is almost never frightened during a tantrum, unless threatened. So, there is no problem of sorting out fear from anger. Instead it is the adult who often feels the most emotionally disturbed—by impulses to hit the child, to throw it out of the house, to dash out and leave the child behind, or to smash the nearest dish.

It is most damaging to frustrate the child's frustration. In practical terms this means it is necessary to distinguish between denying a child's wish, and denying its emotional expression. The first does no lasting harm, although of course the child may be temporarily sad or angry as a result. (This is assuming there is no systematic denial of the child's vital needs.) The second, however, adds insult to injury, in attacking not just the child's wishes or projects, but the child's feelings, which is to say the child itself. So, in principle, I think it is wrong to try and stop a tantrum. I cannot advise people how to bring up their children. Personally, if I know the tantrum is going to drive *me* to my adult equivalent of a tantrum—a sudden explosion of shouting and protest which may be frightening—I tend to pick the child up firmly and carry it to the playroom and close the door. The tantrum can continue in there—but it seldom does. It is important, though, in sending a child to its room for a period of time, that the lights are on, and that there are toys to play with and books to read. You an even bring some to the child, thus showing that you are not being vengeful, or punitive of the child's rage, but simply acting in self-preservation.

Do emotions act against clear thinking?

This question, in one form or another, is quite common and betrays how much society has come to expect a machine-like or computer-like quality in decision-making. But clear or original thinking has probably always been more rare than the dutiful repetition of learned opinions or formulas. It is this latter, mechanical type thinking, which is most threatened by emotion. Remember the old phrase "the excitement of discovery." Or the idea that the best teaching is through excitement. At university I had to study 1,500 lines of an Anglo-

Saxon epic called *Beowulf,* in Old English. Twenty years later
I only remember the first few lines. I remember them because I
can hear them in the voice of J. R. R. Tolkien (of *Lord of the
Rings*) who was normally a dry-as-dust lecturer but would begin
his lecture series by declaiming the first lines of *Beowulf* with
emotion.

This is a scientific age, and science aims for a precision which
rules out emotion. Some scientists retain an emotional enthu-
siasm *about* their work, even if not *in* it. But remember the first
man on the moon's words: "one short step for man, one great
step for mankind." They could have been moving. But Arm-
strong uttered them deadpan, as if feeding the information to a
computer. It seems left to artists and writers to embody human
emotionalism. There is such a thing as poetic thought, a kind of
"feeling thought." Robert Graves has stated: "A poet finds himself caught in some baffling emotional problem, which is of
such urgency that it sends him into a sort of trance. And in this
trance his mind works, with astonishing boldness and precision,
on several imaginative levels at once." Whether poets or not,
many people have experienced some moments where emotional
excitement and mental illumination combine in a rush of in-
sight. Even scientific discoveries are often conceived this way.
But these moments may be denied, or not respected, if the person lacks emotional self-confidence. Instead of computers being
seen as devices which liberate human beings from the drudgery
of endless calculation, "computer-like logic" has become a
model for thought, and even the brain is thought of as a computer in spite of ample evidence it is not. Perhaps this is only a
stage.

But Graves' statement raises another question: could EFA
harm the creative process? If this depends on emotional problems which resolve themselves through the creative work, then
the resolution of the emotional problem might (as Graves put
it in another discussion, of psychoanalysis) "kill the goose that
lays the golden eggs." But I believe emotional problems will
always exist, since life presents us with so many conflicts. What
EFA can do is help sort out the unnecessary emotional confusion which occurs when an emotion presses for expression but

is blocked. Blocked emotion often leads to blocked thinking. If a person is helped to become open to emotion, this means that genuine emotional problems, which involve urgent conflicts of values or needs, are no longer sunk in the swamp of repression, but can emerge to demand resolution in the clear air of conscious thought.

10

Emotional First Aid in Counseling

Non-counselors are invited to read this chapter. It contains no secrets for a closed circle. But it discusses some questions which have come up specifically in seminars I have given on EFA for counselors (which includes psychiatrists, psychologists, psychotherapists, social workers, nurses, etc.). Many counselors have an extensive knowledge of such areas as diagnosis, cognitive problem-solving, biochemistry and medication, family dynamics, sexuality, and so on. But systematic training in direct work with the emotions is non-existent in almost all schools of psychiatry, psychology or social work. After graduation the practitioner is too often left to "wing it" emotionally, and success or failure as a counselor depends on private emotional qualities which the practitioner will have had since before training. This is partly as it should be. No manual of EFA can really teach sensitivity. If the hand on the weeping client's head is hard and cold, and belongs to a contemptuous or rigid person, EFA is merely a mechanical simulation, and the client will know it. But very often the counselor's problem is not a lack of emotional responsiveness, it is a lack of understanding of how emotions *work*—so that attempts to guide a client through an emotional outburst or crisis may be well-intentioned but dangerously inept.

I once attended a training workshop given by a "bioenergetics" therapist whose sensitivity as a person I respect. We were doing one of those exercises, so often forced or silly, where the participants pass one by one in front of the therapist and are encouraged to explore their capacity for anger by shaking their fist and yelling "Get out of my way!" When it was my turn, the therapist adopted a particularly bland, infuriating look of disdain, and I found it easily to mobilize what felt like real anger as I shook my fist and yelled. He then said: This is not convincing. Your forehead is all bunched up. That way your anger can't get out. Open your eyes *wide*, and let me *see* the rage." I was puzzled, since I had been truly burning with anger, but I tried it his way, opening my eyes wide as I yelled. All I felt was a sense of weakness, humiliation, and for the first time a hint of fear. "That's better," he said. "But you could do some work on it."

I was left quite upset by this experience. I had never, being a rather touchy person, felt I had much of a problem with anger. But now I did. My self-confidence was shaken. Some months later I read Darwin and found that all primates, whether apes or humans, do in fact bunch their foreheads in rage. Again, all primates open their eyes wide in fear. So my teacher was simply wrong. But how many other people had had their emotional confidence shaken by his interventions?

On another occasion, in a similar workshop, I was standing near a window minding my own business when another participant came up behind me and pinched both my shoulders and started massaging them vigorously. Almost immediately I had wheeled around with my fist raised and eyes blazing, but as I saw him I checked my anger and we had a good laugh about it. He explained that he had thought I looked sad, and that massaging my shoulders would make me feel better. We agreed that I was "holding anger" in my shoulder muscles. But almost everyone "holds anger" in these muscles, since they are used in hitting out, and become tender when the desire to hit out is repressed. Pinching these muscles almost always triggers anger, and it is not appropriate in helping grief. If the other participant had been in a position of authority (as counselors inevitably are), he could have damaged my emotional self-confidence if he had told me I should not have been angry, or that I should have been trusting enough to give in to his ministrations "to make me feel better." A counselor has the power to make or break a client's emotional self-confidence, and although a healthy person may bounce back quickly, for an emotionally disturbed person the breaking of what confidence there is can be fatal.

How can EFA be used in crisis line counseling?

The basic principles can be applied verbally, although this is of course difficult without visual cues. Any of the measures suggested under the heading of *Contact 2: Touch* can obviously not be applied. Nor, I think, should an attempt be made to give instructions by telephone on how to set up exercises to "get the emotion out."

As crisis line workers know, telephone counseling can be likened to playing a very large but invisible fish which has only been lightly hooked: a combination of strength and delicacy is required, so as not to lose the person at the other end, who can hang up the phone in an instant. Most crisis line workers already apply some verson of the *focus* principle I have discussed with relation to anger, and encourage the caller to be as specific as possible, to concentrate on detail instead of panicking. They also give steady *support* to grief. *Contact*, in the case of fear, is the most difficult when not face to face, but can be partly achieved through the voice. Blocked joy is seldom presented as a problem, but the counselor can be alert to the possibility that anxiety is hiding an unbearable excitement which can be *shared*.

It helps to keep these key words in mind: *support* for grief; *focus* for anger; *contact* for fear; *sharing* for joy. But none of these emotions should be fanned into flame. A basic difference between crisis line counseling and EFA is that on the crisis line, talking for its own sake is encouraged, on the principle that the distressed person needs to discharge emotional tension and can do so through the sometimes long process of expressing his or her troubles verbally to a sympathetic listener. In EFA, where we are in contact with the distressed person, it is useful to try and set talk aside and work to let the emotion be expressed physically. But on a crisis line this is not advisable.

Threats of suicide can be worked through verbally by a skilled counselor who lets the person express his or her troubles, and suggests diversionary activity or further help. All this keeps the emotion low-key. Usually—although there are no firm rules—it takes energy to commit suicide. The person is bursting with pain or emotion, and the suicidal act seems a release from unbearable tension. In therapy, it becomes important to discuss *how* a person is thinking of committing suicide. This tends to defuse the intention, and the person may feel more understood. This should *not* be discussed on the telephone, in my opinion, since there is the small but terrible risk that the person may be stmulated into action instead of this being defused, and it is essential to be in face to face contact in order to monitor for this. But, here, in the interest of understanding, it is worth emphasizing that *there is an emotional and physical logic to suicidal feelings.* The person who wants to blow their brains out may be feeling an intolerable pressure in the head; the one who wants to jump out of a window may already be experiencing a terrified sensation of falling; the one who wants to take pills and "go to sleep" is already deeply exhausted; the one who wants to walk out into the cold sea is already cold and neglected; the one who wants to suffocate already has difficulty breathing. Often a powerful impulse is being directly blocked. One woman, who had cut her wrists when her boyfriend had left her, recalled in therapy: "When he walked out of the room, I went to the window and watched him go down the street, not looking back. I wanted so much to run downstairs after him and grab him and pull him back to me. But I took a knife and slashed my wrists." Here the turning back of the impulse is clear: instead of reaching out with her hands she "cut them off." Another woman who was not suicidal but would sometimes give herself shallow cuts with a knife, jabbing at herself and muttering "No!", eventually found herself taking a knife to her husband and cutting his arm in a quarrel, though again only shallowly: this was the last time she took a knife either to herself or him, since she understood the impulse once it was directed outward, and was able to resolve the conflict behind it.

Since so many suicidal or self-destructive impulses are in fact "retroflections"—turnings back toward the self of an impulse which is murderous or destructive—this underlines the importance of work to focus anger. Suicide is violence against the self. Even EFA can defuse this by providing a channel for the anger expression, so long as the basic guideline is observed of not trying to create anger where no sign of it exists.

This amounts to a warning to crisis line workers. Although you may feel relieved when a depressed and suicidal person begins to show some determination and anger at the other end of a line, this must be considered a *dangerous* situation, since you cannot see the person's face and eyes. Although the words may be angry, even relatively focused, the face may be showing panic. The person could become violent to others, or there could be a sudden switch of direction against the self again, this time with more energy behind it. Everything you can do on the crisis line must be to damp down the person's energy. Even focusing should be discouraged if it gets the person worked up. It may be more helpful to suggest ways in which the person can get some care from a friend, or give it to him or her self. More important even than discussing the other person's emotional situation may be suggestions from you which show solicitousness and care. Most desperate people have stopped eating. They need to feel nourished and mothered, to drink or eat something special (with permission to break a diet, if they are on one), or to have a warm bath and the promise of supportive contact tomorrow. They need reassurance that even their suicidal impulses are the result of natural feelings, and do not have to lead to the act. In all this, the more knowledge you have of emotional functioning, the better. But with threats of suicide, EFA measures should only be employed in face to face counseling.

How can wife-battering be stopped?

It cannot be stopped by EFA, unless in conjunction with therapy. Sado-masochistic dynamics are too intricate, and the breakdown of anger into violence has gone too far.

The only use for EFA in this circumstance is in dealing with the feelings of a wife who has left a husband: counselors in half-way houses for such women have been frequent attenders at EFA courses. What disturbs these counselors most is the way many women go back to the abusing husband again and again. This is often masochism—which the counselors can easily see. But it is sometimes genuine love and sexual attraction—which the counselors often have difficulty in acknowledging. In either case, EFA can work best with the woman's anger *if it is there already* in some form. Unfortunately many counselors are operating with an ideology: the abused woman *should* be angry. No doubt. But sometimes she is *not.* It is one of the most damaging mistakes in counseling to assume that everyone has anger to burn. Whether they do or not is a question of character structure. The basic principle that EFA works to help the expression of whatever emotion is already present, can be followed in all work with abused wives. The counselor has to put aside expectations, and do a good job of helping the woman express her grief, anger, or fear—in the order in which they present themselves. The woman has had enough of not having the order of her feelings respected. The good counselor knows this.

How does EFA handle phobias?

There is a division of opinion in psychotherapy about phobias. On one side are those, mainly behaviorists (but recently joined by practitioners of "neuro-linguistic programming") who see each phobia as a specific problem to be worked on in isolation. On the other side are those, mainly practitioners of various psychodynamic approaches, who see the phobia as a symptom of a larger disturbance, or as a displacement of another, deeper fear. I belong in the second camp. But the first, or mechanistic, camp has on its side the fact that its methods usually *work*—for a while. A person may be bullied out of a phobia by the use of punishment; bored out of it by desensitizing or deconditioning; or have its cognitive elements smoothly tied together by the conjuring trick of "re-programming." But it usually comes back within a few months, or a new phobia takes its place—which can then be mechanistically treated again in isolation. The problem becomes like a Hydra, the serpent with many heads which grew a new one each time one of them was lopped off. Only, the second camp would maintain, if the body of the Hydra is dealt with, will the heads stop being replaced. This may be a matter for therapy. But in EFA terms, the body of the Hydra is *fear itself*—though the heads are *angry*.

In other words, the phobia is a reduction of the fear to a narrow focus which is obsessive and rage-like. Remember the example of the man in the lumberyard. He seems to have had a phobia of snakes. He therefore pounded a harmless snake to death. Since he eliminates all snakes on sight, he will hardly be able to explore the origins of his fear. Though not all phobias lead to outbursts of rage or attack, many do. An example might be a man who is phobic of homosexuals, because of a deep fear that he might be one himself, who takes any opportunity to attack a weak homosexual and beat him up. Even where the phobia does not seem to contain an element of anger, when a person is asked to describe the object of the phobia an angry expression may appear. In another case the person may break out into a cold sweat and "freeze." But this is, I maintain, largely a fear of his or her own anger: it is as if a layer of fear covers anger which in turn covers fear.

Take agoraphobia, the fear of crowds. The agoraphobic will be afraid to leave the house. But she (agoraphobics are usually women, as paranoiacs are usually men) will often, when questioned, reveal quite a contempt for crowds. They jostle, they smell, they are crude and mindless. As the agoraphobic talks about crouds, anger may begin to emerge—and the fear of her own anger. Or take a phobia about dirt. What is the facial expression of the woman scrubbing the sink for the tenth time, or the man putting on rubber gloves to take out the garbage? It is one of disdain and disgust, in which fear is visible in raised eyebrows, but anger is visible in tight jaw and snarling lips.

Even basic EFA procedures are thus a help with phobias, because eventually they bring out the anger as well as the fear. Ideally, these can be dealt with in order: first anger, then fear.

The more angry the person can consciously become with the object of the phobia, the more the way is cleared to find out what the deep fear is about—although this is an issue for therapy, since it may be mixed in a complex tangle of longings and deprived needs. It is as if once the Hydra's angry heads are encouraged to lunge out far enough, the poor fearful body becomes exposed.

Can EFA help with the consequences of sexual abuse?

This subject is topical, because of the increasing attention given not only to the victims of sexual assault or rape, but to the victims of sexual abuse within families. At the beginning of the century Freud was considered to have a dirty mind because he showed interest in his patients' stories of sexual abuse by relatives, notably of girls by fathers. Freud, at least, took these stories seriously, but he considered most of them to be fantasies expressing disguised incest wishes. In recent years, in a period of greater outspokenness and unremitting research into sexuality, it has become clear that most such stories are not fantasies but truth. This is no surprise to any therapist who works intensively with the emotions of troubled people. I would estimate that three in ten of my female clients have been in one way or another sexually abused by fathers or elder brothers, as have about one in twenty of my male clients.

In the case of rape, attention is being rightly given to ways of supporting victims and rendering the aftermath less traumatic. The emphasis is on reassurance. But this cannot be enough. I have had no experience with "rape relief centers," but in therapy I have had several women work through the emotional consequences of rape in the past. Women who have already established a solid sexual life at the time of the rape adjust better to their anger than those less experienced—in the sense that although their anger may be strong, it does not necessarily become evoked by all men. But where rape is the first, or one of the first sexual experiences of men, the rage is more diffuse. As always, it is a matter of how far the rage is focused. In some cases it is retroflected: the woman blames herself, and her femininity, for seductiveness. This blame must be turned *outward,* to the person who has abused her, even if this is a person who "should" be loved, such as a relative.

The most damaging situation occurs when the rage is diffuse, a mixture of fear and anger at men and at sexuality itself, which is then repressed. On the surface the woman becomes compliant, even seductive, and highly interested in seeking out sexual encounters—but underneath she is repressing a generalized rage, she is manipulative of men, her sexual seductiveness is a testing maneuver, and she experiences no deep genital pleasure. Physically, the abdomen and pelvis are tight, and nervous or jumpy when touched, with the breath kept high in the chest. In therapy, the first emotion to come through, when the controlled exterior cracks, is crying; but rage is not far behind. The emotional and physical picture is similar in most cases of sexual abuse within the family, but there is more to work through: the woman's self-confidence has often been crushed by the brutal and systematic exercise of power by a man whom she has wanted to love.

It is worth remembering that while the use of EFA methods in these cases to focus anger may bring out many horrible and upsetting details, and at the time it may seem as if all hope of the person being able to re-establish a loving sexuality is lost; in fact, the opposite is true. Bringing out rage at a specific man clears the way for the appreciation of other men who are different. There is no need for a deliberate reminder, "Not all men are like that." The realization will come on its own. As always, it is the repression of emotion which is most dangerous. It is rather like the process when you meet a new person, "A," who reminds you strongly of another, "B." This will occur every time you meet. But once you tell "A" he or she reminds you of "B," the similarity fades. Suddenly you are aware of "A" in his or her own right, and the presence of "B" falls away. When a woman has been abused by "X," it is only when her anger at this man has been fully brought out that she begins to be confident that "Y" and "Z" are *not* "X." Again, the key word must be *focus:* the anger has to be directed at "X" and at no one else. To encourage a generalized anger at men, sex, or the world, is both morally irresponsible and emotionally damaging.

When a boy has been abused sexually by a man, the situation is similar, but with the added problem that if the boy becomes diffusely angry (or represses anger) at all men, this makes it impossible for him to become fully a man.

How do emotional blocks effect a person's world view?

Some version of this question is usually asked by psychologists or others with an interest in perception and cognition. I have already suggested that cognitive problems are part of the superstructure over an emotional base. Modern psychology demonstrates more and more that perception is a process of unconscious selection of some focused items from a diffuse field of impressions, and I would suggest that this selection process is largely based in the person's emotional attitudes and expectations. Both cognition and perception tend to reorganize themselves spontaneously if therapy, or some other intensely felt event, has produced emotional change.

I have had participants in seminars do an experiment which I first developed for a lecture to an art therapy conference. (Some of my clients in therapy have been enrolled simultaneously in an art therapy program, and watching their paintings change during the course of therapy has stimulated my interest in this link between emotional and perceptual change.) The experiment is loosely based on the standard psychological "house-tree-person" test. This is a projective test in which the details of the three items indicate the person's attitudes to the self and others. In my experiment, the details are unimportant because each drawing is done very quickly, in 20–30 seconds. The reader is invited to try it for him or herself:

Take four sheets of blank paper, and a strong pencil or crayon. You will be asked to draw a rough sketch of a house, a tree and a person on each sheet, each time as fast as you can, and following these instructions:

Do not pause between sheets to inspect your work. Take the first sheet.

1. Begin to pant high in your chest, gasping *in* as much air

as possible. At the same time let your jaw drop open wide; open your eyes as wide as you can; and raise your eyebrows as high as you can. *Maintain* this breathing pattern and expression, and *draw.*

Put the first sheet aside and take the second.

2. Breathe *out* harshly and quickly a few times, making a sound and pushing out as much air as possible. Keep doing this. At the same time, stick your jaw and lower lip forward; narrow your eyes; and frown so that a knot is formed between your eyes. Now, *draw.*

Put the second sheet aside and take the third.

3. Reduce your breathing to a *minimum.* Let your jaw hang open. Let your eyes go *blank* as you look at the paper, defocusing completely. *Draw.*

Put the third sheet aside and take the fourth.

4. Become your normal self again. Pay no special attention to your breathing or facial expression. *Draw.*

If you want to try this experiment, please do so before reading further.

The reader will have recognized that step 1 is an imitation of fear, step 2 of anger. Most people do recognize this, although it is not spelled out in the instructions. Step 3 is a "spaced out" expression. Step 4, normal.

In seminars I have the participants compare their own and each others' drawings, if they feel comfortable doing so. The reader can simply spread all four drawings out and compare them. *This is not a personality test.* It is an exploration of how emotion, as evoked in a simulation, can effect perception. However, in looking at your pictures you may reach some conclusions about yourself. Do not take these too seriously. But you may, for example, have noticed that your step 4 "normal" drawing is more similar to one in particular of your previous drawings. This may indicate your predominant emotional "tone." You may find the drawings rather uniform, which may indicate some anxiety at abandoning yourself to emotion. Or you may have found a particular expression anxiety-provoking or difficult.

Generally, step 1 produces a drawing in which lines are disconnected; the three items become looming and large; the forms are rounded or oblong with few sharp edges; and pencil pressure is light. This is the way the world is perceived in fear. Occasionally though, the drawing is different, with tighter, smaller figures, and a harder pencil pressure. In this case, you might ask yourself if you have been able to imitate the expression fully, and if you tend to fight against a fearful attitude with an attitude of attack.

Generally, step 2 produces a drawing in which lines are straight; the three items are reduced and compressed; the forms are sharp and angular; and pencil pressure is heavy. All this is consistent with the "attack" of the expression. It is the way the world tends to be perceived in anger. Occasionally this sharpness does not come through, and the focus remains rounded or vague. You might look at whether you had difficulty with the attack expression.

Generally, step 3 produces a drawing which is more similar to 1 than to 2, but with an increased fuzziness or vagueness, or with a tendency to fragmentation, or to abstraction or geometry. The "blanking" of the eyes cuts you off somewhat from reality. Whereas step 1 evoked a panicky kind of fear, step 3 is more a "fright paralysis."

It may be useful for counselors to have their clients do this experiment. But, remember, it is not a test, and no diagnostic conclusions should be made—although, of course, any increased knowledge of the client can support or render questionable a diagnosis. I find it unnecessary to discuss the drawings with the person much more than I have been doing here. It is often an interesting *experience* from which the person will draw his or her own conclusions.

11

A Note on Self Help and Professional Help

It has been clear from classes in EFA that many participants are primarily interested in EFA as a method of self help. Then, why not call it Emotional Self Help? Because in directing these methods of help toward others, they become more clear, and problems in their use become more apparent. It is easier to deduce methods of self help from a knowledge of how to help others than vice-versa. EFA includes emotional self help. In the chapters of this book that treat the four basic emotions, the sections on Experiencing consist of simulations that are, in effect, self-help exercises. Other sections on Expression, Distress, Provocation, and Resolution are as valid for self help as for helping others. The sections on Contact 1 and 2, Problems, and Emergency can also be read from a self-help point of view, and perhaps as an aid in clarifying what kind of help it is possible to ask from other people.

There are limitations to self help. Reich compared the idea that a person could do self therapy to the story of the man who tried to pull himself out of a swamp by his own hair. Self therapy, or self analysis, is full of self deception. But Emotional First Aid opens the possibility of a more honest contact between people. Since more than one person is involved, some emotional resolution or increased self knowledge can result. More importantly, if we are able to be supportive of people with whom we have personal relationships, our contact has more energy and is less undermined by the pressure of undischarged emotional tension from outside sources.

The psychoanalyst Eric Berne remarked, 'Love is nature's therapy.' Although I work as a therapist, I do not believe that everyone needs therapy. And I do not believe in the idea that once started, therapy never finishes, that it is part of a perpetual process of personal growth. I know many people who keep growing and facing life problems without any need for therapy. On the other hand, if life problems cannot be resolved because of chronic emotional blocks, therapy is a possible resource. And a personal therapy is essential for any therapist or counselor. If you feel chronically stuck in some area of your life, have no shame about seeking the help of a therapist. But make sure that he or she has, in the course of training, undergone therapy 'from the other end.'

Seeking professional help is not as simple as going to a psychiatrist or psychologist. Psychiatrists (physicians, M.D.s, who have undergone further specialized training in the field of mental illness) are usually oriented toward treating emotional problems through medication. Their training also influences them strongly to see emotional problems in terms of illness or disorder, which is sometimes but not always valid. For some psychiatrists, an attempt to understand the patient through psychotherapy is limited to a preliminary interview, after which drugs are prescribed. Others, however, have become skilled therapists, usually through nonmedical training with an institute or school that specializes in one of the many forms of psychotherapy or psychoanalysis.

Psychologists (usually with a Ph.D. or M.A. degree) often have no training in psychotherapy, but are experts in human behavior, development, learning theory, or the behavior of rats. The popular Bob Newhart image of a psychologist usually applies only to what are called 'clinical psychologists.' They too have often received much of their practical training from private institutes, outside the universities.

To confuse the issue further, the popular image of a psychologist applies also to many counselors who have done their formal training in the field of Education. In fact, in almost all universities, the most systematic training in techniques of psychotherapy is to be found not in psychology departments but in departments of education, counseling, or social work.

There are many excellent therapists who have no formal training in either medicine or psychology, but who have trained privately. Most have a preliminary academic degree in a field associated with human behavior.

All this means that a good therapist may be a psychiatrist, a physician, a psychologist, a counselor, or a social worker. If you seek to work on your problems with a therapist, your choice of where to look is probably determined by your prior reading, financial considerations (therapy with a physician or psychiatrist is usually covered by insurance; with the other categories this is less likely), and your conception of what kind of background you want your therapist to have.

To find a therapist who will work with the emotions along the lines discussed in this book is not always easy. Reichian therapists (sometimes known as orgone therapists, or as 'orgonomists') are sparsely scattered. Various neo-Reichian therapies, such as Bioenergetic Analysis, are oriented to the view of the emotions as structured in the body musculature, but use an approach based on stressful exercises, which are not necessarily sensitive to the individual's needs. Ordinary 'talk therapy' may in fact be more in contact with the individual. Some therapists from the various categories mentioned above who have been trained in 'family therapy' are sensitive to the emotions and are used to facing the dynamics of relationships.

My own bias is in favor of Reichian therapy. But all kinds of therapy, including Reichian therapy, can be manipulative in the hands of a practitioner who is not adequately trained or who has not worked through his or her own emotional blocks.

Under the circumstances, the prospective patient or client has the right to exercise great care in the choice of a therapist, to question the therapist extensively in the preliminary interview, and to stop the therapy unilaterally if it becomes impossible to resolve through discussion with the therapist whatever doubts may emerge about the therapy. No therapist, whether psychiatrist, psychologist, or counselor, is worth working with if he or she is not ready to answer the following questions:

1) Where and for how long did you receive your training in therapy?

2) Have you undergone a personal therapy? With whom?

3) Do you work directly with the emotions? How?

If you sense any evasiveness in a therapist's answers to these questions, or if you find that you simply do not like him or her, seek another therapist. There is no harm in 'shopping around.' On the other hand, don't expect a therapist to have to charm you into making a commitment. A good therapist will not necessarily give you an easy time in a preliminary interview. He or she too will be trying to find out how serious you are. But he or she should answer your questions.

Some therapists may agree to a trial period. You might 'contract' for three or four sessions, so that you can find out what kind of work is involved, while the therapist has at least an initial commitment from you. After such a trial period, you should have a basic understanding of each other, and of how far you may want to proceed. Of course, you are free to stop when you want. It might be part of your contract with the therapist, though, that you will, at that time, take a session to discuss your reasons for leaving therapy. This will be an indication that you are not simply running away. Follow your instincts. But it will not be an easy voyage. If you take it, good luck.

Suggested Further Reading

Area

The dynamics of the emotions:

Darwin, Charles. *The Expression of the Emotions in Man and Animals.* University of Chicago Press, 1965.

Reich, Wilhelm. *Character Analysis.* New York: Simon & Schuster, Inc, 1974. (Chapter 15: 'The Expressive Language of the Living').

Haldane, Sean. *Applied Reichian Therapy.* New York: Irvington Publishers, 1981. (Section 1: 'The Formation of Character Armor').

Childbirth and mothering:

Kitzinger, Sheila. *The Experience of Childbirth.* New York: Taplinger Publishing Co., 1972.

Newton, Niles. *Maternal Emotions.* New York. 1955.

Pryor, Karen. *Nursing Your Baby.* New York: Harper & Row, 1973.

Childhood and adult needs:

Bowlby, John. *Attachment and Loss.* Basic Books, 1969.

Montagu, Ashley. *Touching.* New York: Columbia University Press, 1971.

Index